"This is a refreshing look at the puzzling world faced by today's teens and the moms and dads who are trying to guide them. Incorporating advances in neuroscience, psychiatrist David Dawson clearly describes how teen brains work and offers practical advice to baffled parents in a fun and relaxing style. At the same time, he helps parents have confidence in their innate good instincts and solid understanding of their own children. Also included are significant behavioural warning signs that may be the early stages of serious mental illness. Readers will appreciate his friendly accounts of his own problems as a dad; his humility, always welcome in a psychiatrist, adds to the appeal of this helpful guidebook."
  - Susan Inman

What they say about Dawson's other books:

"This is one of only two books I have read in the field that I try to make sure everyone reads..." - Susan Stefan

"This excellent, clearly written and incredibly useful book is a must have for any Adult Community Mental Health Service"
-   F. Lange

"Last Rights is simply a gem..."   - Vancouver Sun

"Dawson's vital characters and the ambience of his city and institutional scenes earn him respect as the author of both a superb mystery and a compelling novel." – Publishers Weekly

'This is a fast paced book with a terrific idea at its heart."
-   The Globe and Mail

"...lets us inside the heads and hearts of a few wonderful and fully formed characters..."   - The Boston Globe

The Adolescent Owner's Manual

The Adolescent Owner's Manual

David Laing Dawson, MD

Bridgeross Communications
Dundas, Canada

Copyright 2010 © David Laing Dawson

Library and Archives Canada Cataloguing in Publication

Dawson, David Laing
        The adolescent owner's manual / David Laing
Dawson.

ISBN 978-0-9866522-0-2

        1. Teenagers.   2. Parent and teenager. 3.
        Adolescent psychology.
I. Title.

HQ799.15.D38 2010   306.874   C2010-905662-0

Cover Illustration by David Shaw

Bridgeross Communications
Dundas, Ontario, Canada

Also by David Laing Dawson

Fiction:

Last Rights

Double Blind

Essondale

The Intern

Slide in all Direction

Don't Look Down

Non-fiction:

Schizophrenia in Focus

Relationship Management of the Borderline Patient

Film & Video:

Who Cares

Manic

My Name is Walter James Cross

Painting with Tom, David, and Emily

Cutting for Stone

The Pen, The Brush, and Recovery

For all those parents who now have to contend with cell phones, video games, videocams, texting, sexting, twitter, Facebook, MSN, You Tube, porn sites, nose rings, tongue studs, tattoos, as well as Sex, Drugs, Cars, and Rock and Roll.

Contents

Preface

Let's start with Socrates. The parents of each generation despair of their teenagers, and we know it goes back at least as far as Socrates. What he said was, "Children today are tyrants. They contradict their parents, gobble their food, and tyrannize their teachers." And those kids did not have cell phones, MP3 players, MSN, Facebook, automobiles, and Heavy Metal Music.

And then we have Shakespeare. I don't know why 'Romeo and Juliet' is taught in High School English but it is. We were told this is a tale about warring families, controlling patriarchs, and the pure love of a boy and a girl conquering all. But is it? Both of these children die before the play is over.

My grade 12 English teacher had a sense of humor. I'm sure it was not mere coincidence that he asked me to read, in front of the class, the Romeo part, and my then girlfriend, the Juliet part.

"Put more feeling in it," he said. "You're reading in a monotone."

Sure. I was lucky to get the words at all, what with sweat dripping in my eyes and a blush swelling my lips. But we were four years older than Romeo and Juliet and we had at least gained sufficient maturity to feel embarrassment, something apparently alien to Shakespeare's younger characters.

We were told Romeo and Juliet was a story of "star-crossed lovers". But it can also be read as the story of the conflict between our biological imperative to widen and enrich the gene pool and to defend the nest, the home, the tribe, the community, and the status

1

quo. It can be read as the futility, the tragedy of tribalism and the poetic glory of pure and simple love.

But isn't it also a story about two 14 year old kids who get way in over their heads while mom and dad are not paying quite enough attention? Their adolescent intrigue, their soap opera romance, their teenage fantasy, is allowed to flourish unbridled (or inconsistently bridled). Their peers join in the grand concoction. Their lives spin out of control, and they both make the kind of decisions only adolescents make. (Well, adolescents or adults with serious mental disorders)

There is that whole Montague/Capulet rivalry stuff, but so what? Had the lovers in question been 22 or 24 they might have left home and moved to Buffalo and opened a hemp store, or a tattoo parlour, and then reconciled with their families a few years later. Or Romeo might have overcome some test to win the respect of Juliet's father. Or the more sensible mothers may have intervened. Or they might have immigrated to Australia, or hitchhiked around Europe. And Mr. Shakespeare could have written this play as a Romantic Comedy. But it is written as a Tragedy, with fourteen year-olds making life-altering decisions based on their own, nascent, very limited understanding of themselves in the world.

Our teens get out of control, they get in trouble; they represent the future and they carry the burdens of the past. They give us pleasure and drive us crazy. They make terrible decisions based on strange notions of invulnerability, entitlement, and the self-evident truth of their feelings. Most of them will find their way safely into adulthood, which (as mentioned many times on these pages) does not really arrive until age 22, 23, 24 or thereabouts.

This book is about averting the tragedies of adolescence and enjoying the comedies, and of both parents and their children

2

surviving adolescence with no more than a rueful grin and a few stories to tell their friends, other parents, and their grandchildren.

It can be awfully difficult with adolescents, to distinguish the behaviours caused by raging hormones combined with underdeveloped frontal lobes, the momentary stupidity, the passing phase, from those behaviours caused by a developing illness. So a chapter will be devoted to this: when might it be wise to seek the help of a professional?

I. Getting to Know Your Adolescent

Numerous books and chapters of books have been written about that phase of human development we call adolescence. They describe developmental psychology, personality theory, studies of adolescent behaviour, and family functioning. They explain the developmental tasks of adolescence, the struggle to define one's identity, one's independent sense of self. Surprisingly, some studies show that most young people negotiate this phase of their lives without excessive anxiety, conflict, confusion, depression, or outrageous behaviour. Still, adolescence can be difficult for both adolescents and their parents, and these difficulties can range from a long-remembered embarrassing moment, to a family breakdown, or a life altering decision.

We can all remember moments of excruciating confusion, avoidance, embarrassment, fear and uncertainty during our adolescence. Some of us still blame our parents for this. For most of us, adolescence remained an internal experience that did not, at least not that often, spin out-of-control.

We avoided lengthy discussions with our parents; we gave attitude; we assumed world-weary postures; we knew all we needed to know; we avoided anything that might challenge our fragile developing sense of self; we pushed the boundaries but seemed to know when things were going a little too far.

If we were lucky, someone among our group of friends might say, "That's a stupid idea." Fortunately we didn't have enough money to buy the quantities of Vodka that could prove lethal. We drove our cars when we shouldn't have driven our cars, but there was less traffic then, and fewer distractions. We might purposely get low marks, in order to appear cool, be one-of-the-guys, but still, at least, we passed the course. We might skip school a few times but not to the point of expulsion, and we might disobey curfew but not by so much that the old man would take away the car keys for life.

Of course it could be that those of us who survived adolescence were just lucky.

A small group of 18 year olds, to celebrate the end of High School, loaded cars with cases of beer, cheap wine, a little food and sleeping bags, and drove to a fishing cabin sitting just above high tide on a secluded west coast road on Vancouver Island. They walked the beach; they cooked; they ate; they talked; they drank. And then they drank some more. And some more. And some more.

Fifty feet from the cabin's door the Pacific surf crashed against the pebbled beach. One among the group, destined to become a teacher, seemed to fully grasp the nature of adolescence. He dumped a glass of wine over the head of another boy, simply because, as he explained it, he felt like doing it, and it was possible to do it. "Why not?" was his guiding wisdom. Maybe a food fight ensued. I don't remember. But I do remember that at about two in the morning, under a bright moon, this group of boys decided to launch a boat into the surf. Five drunken teenage boys, a fifteen-foot outboard, four-foot waves rolling into shore, the moon smiling down upon us. We made several attempts, but the waves were too high and we were too sloppy and uncoordinated. I have always thought it a great piece of luck that we failed.

We dragged the boat back to shore and continued our drinking. The next day, suffering the kind of hangover one gets from drinking copious amounts of sweet wine and beer, we swore off alcohol. For each of us this resolution lasted, possibly, a week or two.

Years later, one of the group, who eventually became a judge, remembered that moment somewhat differently. In his memory we did not try very hard to launch our skiff. We collectively held back at the last moment. Perhaps one of us feigned a slip and a splash. Perhaps we all held back from full effort, because somewhere in the back of our brains we knew this was really not a good idea. But it certainly could have played out differently.

Every long hot summer weekend teenagers have boating accidents and drown. Or they simply jump in turbulent water best enjoyed from shore. Perhaps it was a matter of luck for ourselves, or some among us were just smart and mature enough to register, "This is not a safe thing to do", or we had each received adequate parenting and a voice in our heads was saying, "If you don't drown trying something so stupid you'll be grounded for six months."

Of course, as parents, we don't want to squelch risk- taking altogether. Without some adolescent and post-adolescent risk-taking we wouldn't have personal computers at our fingertips, and Microsoft to fuel them; we wouldn't have astonishing art, remarkable novels, an ever-changing music. We do need some people approaching life saying "Why not?" rather than "Why?"

In his later years George Bernard Shaw described himself in youth as an "extremely disagreeable and undesirable" young man, "not at all reticent of diabolical opinion," while inwardly "suffering….from simple cowardice and horribly ashamed of it."

6

At age twenty he took a risk and left the life in business planned for him by his family and began to write.

In a way, GBS captures many adolescents with his phrases "extremely disagreeable, undesirable, not at all reticent of diabolical opinion, while inwardly ashamed."

My father once commented, regarding his three children, "You were all easy to raise." That was probably true, though I'm sure he didn't know the full story of our adventures with surf and boat, all night beach parties, and drunk driving.

It is certainly true that some adolescents are easier to raise than others. Some of this difference may be purely a function of genetics, of biology and inherited temperament. Studies of Chimpanzee adolescents in the wild show that some stay close to home, rise in the pecking order, dine with family, mate within the tribe, while others, against all odds and rising stress levels, even while taking beatings and being chased away, persist in pursuing membership and mating with the tribe across the river. Although even these adventurous chimps, when badly injured, come home to die.

My daughter was off and running on a backpacking world journey the moment she got the chance. My son ignored a free ticket to Australia to stay within his neighbourhood.

Some adolescents need to be encouraged, cajoled, even pushed into new and different experiences, into joining and playing something other than a video game. Some need to be held back until ready, until their knowledge, perception, judgement, and problem solving have caught up with their energies and impulses. Some will sail through this phase of development needing little more than a safe home, a well-stocked refrigerator, and a little encouragement or corrective advice now and then. Some will need a watchful eye and a firm hand. Many need an almost superhuman fine balance of love, tolerance, understanding, freedom, control, structure, and discipline.

As a parent you will make mistakes. You will worry about the wrong things. You will criticize and lecture when you should have said nothing more than, "Uh huh." You will not act when you should have acted because you are either tired, have other things on your mind, don't want a fight just now, are too angry, or don't want to upset your spouse. Fortunately, adolescents usually give us a second and third chance to be good parents.

We also make mistakes with our adolescents because we simply do not understand them. One moment we have a kid who wants a smile and a hug, the next moment he seems irritated by our very existence. One moment he is showing us how to use a search engine with great facility, the next he says something really, really stupid. One moment she's having a great time playing hide and seek with a young cousin, the next she wants to go out on Friday night dressed in inadequate clothing. One moment she's talking of her plans for the summer, the next all you get is, "Whatever." He is exposed to far more information than any generation before and yet he seems to know nothing. She is writing poetry. This is good. But though she lives a comfortable existence in middle class suburbia, her poetry is full of morbid fear and self-loathing. He is drawing. This is good. But he's drawing guns and tanks and missiles and planes and explosions. His parents are teachers. His background is Catholic. Yet he doesn't know the name of the current Prime Minister and he's fascinated with the possible existence of the anti-Christ and the significance of 666.

The sixteen-year-old boy has been struggling with school and surly with his parents. He is reticent, difficult to engage. He looks depressed. Or maybe he's just sulking. I search for some way to engage him, with his

8

mother present. He's been working on an invention. His
eyes light up when he talks about it. He becomes
animated. Like all good inventors he has noticed an
inconvenience and figured a way to overcome it. He
explains in that particularly teenage manner of false
starts, half sentences, and limited vocabulary. The
problem is, he tells me, you gotta go to the refrigerator,
open it, take out a bowl of something, and carry it over to
the counter and open the microwave to put it in. Lots of
wasted steps there. So his invention, which will make him
millions he figures, is to build the microwave right into
the refrigerator. Voila.

I give it some thought.

Their brains are in flux. The parts that support impulses, energy, sex and aggression, are developing faster than the parts that provide brakes, inhibitions, second thoughts, the ability to hypothesize outcome and consequences. Their brains are ready to explore relationships, figure out patterns of social organization, create habits of behaviour that will allow them to succeed in the adult world, and yet they only want to talk and play with one another. They seem to respond with great sympathy, tears and anguish over a wounded bird, an injured puppy, yet care not a whit for your upcoming surgery, fever, arthritis, lay off. She may form strong opinions about good causes: global warming, saving the forests and the whales, conservationism, vegetarianism, but does she have to be so nasty about it all? You thought your son would be a challenge, but it turns out his younger sister is the one. You thought if you raised your boys and your girls with the same expectations, gender differences would be minimal, yet they are behaving so differently.

You hear yourself saying what your mother said (well, at least what my mother said over and over again): "It would take you a quarter of the time and energy you use avoiding doing what I've asked you to do, to actually do it." This is called appealing to reason. It never seems to work with teenagers.

They can be delightful and puzzling. One moment you can see yourself in your son, the next you're sure he was born of Alien invaders.

When trying to understand other people we tend to assume they think like we do, they process information the same way, they bring the same assumptions to the table, their world view is similar to ours, and they should, at the very least, listen to the logic of self-interest. Even with adults these assumptions can let us down: witness much failed foreign policy. With teenagers it almost always lets us down. They do think differently than we do. They process information a little differently, and some of their assumptions about the world and themselves are not the same as ours.

To understand adolescents we need to do away with the notion that they are simply adults-in-the-making.

Over time, observation of teenage behaviour in various contexts has led me to the following list of truisms. Recent studies of adolescent brain development provide a neurological foundation for most of these observations.

II. Performance and Limitations of Your Adolescent

1. Limitations

Your teenager's brain is not mature. Full brain maturity is reached about age 22. Until then the parts of the brain that house the following abilities **are not fully developed**:

1.1 The ability to **empathize** (with the exception of a strong protective emotional response to small furry big-eyed creatures, which is not empathy but rather a genetic trait common to all humans, including Pamela Anderson, Heather Mills and Brigitte Bardot). We are all programmed to respond warmly and protectively to infants of our own species, and their look-a-likes. And when these particular genes first developed our ancestors and their babies were quite furry. Empathy is different. Empathy is the ability to put yourself (imagine yourself) in another's shoes, someone not small, cute, and furry, someone more like your mother or father, a teacher, or a Newfoundland fisherman trying to feed his four children.

The single parent on limited budget has just had a hysterectomy. She signs out of the hospital early, taking a taxi, because she doesn't want to leave her sixteen year-old daughter home alone any longer than necessary. The cab pulls up. The mother gets out and walks slowly up the pathway to her small house. Just inside the front door, exhausted, holding her sore abdomen, she is confronted by her daughter. The child is dressed in her party finest. She tells her mother it's about time she got home. She's late. And can I have that twenty dollars you promised me. The mother wearily fetches a bill from her purse and the girl is gone.

11

I tell the mother that her daughter has a few more years for her brain to develop the capacity for empathy, and to lose some of its egocentricity, and then we talk of ways the mother might nudge that process along. Of course the mother is hoping some counselling might do the trick, but really it is a parent's job. Not that you can teach empathy, but perhaps by example, and by exposing your child to situations beyond her comfort zone, a parent can hurry the process along. But it is foolish to expect empathy of a 16 year-old. Enjoy it and reward it in the rare moments it occurs.

I had occasion to talk with a newly married woman in her early twenties. Her parents were visiting with their severely handicapped son. She tells me she was horrible to him and to them as a teenager. She hated him. Her parents had always included her brother, taken him with them everywhere. She had hated them for that as well. And then something happened, something internal. And now she admires her parents, loves them for their devotion to their disabled son. She even likes her brother.

Empathy can develop earlier; and when it does it can cause warmth to envelope a parent's heart: There is a hearing impaired kid on your son's hockey team. Your son has been asked to buddy with him, help him through those hockey moments when hearing whistles and other sounds is important. Your son takes to this task whole-heartedly, perhaps missing those moments he could show off for the NHL scouts he imagines sitting behind the bench. Very nice. And you might have a nice talk, an open discussion with your teen one day, and find, indeed, she is displaying a heart warming empathy for others, a hopeful beginning. But the next day it might disappear in a torrent of "What about me?" and "You're being so unfair."

Every year or so one reads of a 12 or 13 year old who has taken up a cause, collecting funds for the children of Darfur, for example. This is a good thing, and it seems to speak of the very

12

early development of strong empathy. But it is probably not empathy. It is probably obsession - a child's tendency to obsess, this time not about his Pokemon cards, or thunderstorms, or the newest video game he would like to own, but about some images he and his parents watched on a Sunday evening newscast. Don't use this child's behaviour as a touchstone and despair of your own adolescent's thoughtlessness. The capacity for true empathy takes time to develop. Take pleasure in it when it happens.

1.2 The ability to **hypothesize the possible short and long term consequences** of various behaviours, including lying. For the most part, teenagers live in the moment. A gravel road, a sharp curve. Can this be negotiated at 100 K per hour? 120 K? 140K? What is the upper limit? There is a way to find out, if we ignore, or rather can't imagine, the consequences. Can one jump from a roof into a swimming pool? Why not sneak out of the house, catch a bus to Chicago to meet your Internet buddy, the one who seems to understand you so completely?

So expect them to do things, and to talk one another into doing things, that a sane adult would not do, this sane adult having imagined the possible outcomes of said activity.

Living in the moment and having limited capacity to imagine outcome may explain the tendency for teenagers to lie. Which they do.

A common adolescent lie is the **path of least resistance lie**. Its goal is to avoid unpleasantness at this moment. Adults usually (not always though – an exception being those moments when you are asked by the police officer if you know at what speed you were driving) take a second to consider the likelihood of the lie unravelling in the next 12 hours. Not so for adolescents (and addicts for that matter, though for different reasons). If the lie can buy 12 hours avoiding the consequences for doing exactly what they are denying having done, even if the consequences will be doubled because of the lie, they will use the lie. The future might be the title of a Leonard Cohen song or something traded on Wall Street, but otherwise, in their lives, it is a very fuzzy concept. It is not something to be considered now when more important things are at hand, like getting on Facebook to tell their 250 closest friends who they saw sitting together at McDonalds.

Studies show that indeed time does move more rapidly for adults, more slowly for youth. Having had to sit with nothing to do, or even with something to do, and then being asked how much time has passed, the adolescent will vastly overestimate, as in, "I've been waiting for hours." and "Are we there yet?" So the future, for a teen, is a long way off. There is time for variables to change the otherwise predictable. A Tornado could strike and carry off the liquor cabinet before Dad has a chance to count the bottles. So, no, I swear to God, Dad, I haven't touched your bourbon.

Actually, lying comes so naturally to teens, it, the lie, in and of itself, should not cause overmuch concern. As a parent, you need to verify the story, and confront the lie, but really it is the act that necessitated the lie that is the important issue. If a teen steals, be it father's bourbon, change from atop the dresser, or worse, when that teen is confronted, the initial lie, the path of least resistance lie, is as natural as rain in April. It would be nice if it didn't happen, but it is natural. It is the stealing that needs to be caught and punished in appropriate fashion. I mention this because some parents often seem more concerned about the lying than the deed itself. I think this is because the teen often continues to deny despite being confronted with blatant evidence, and this can be very annoying, even insulting.

Well, the teen has a few more years to learn an appropriate set of rules for civilized adult lying, when it may be a kindness to avoid the complete truth, or to spin the story, when lying would be futile or self-serving, and how the truth can serve him well. It is the

14

stealing itself, or the drunk driving, or the Oxycontin party that needs to be corrected now. As Judge Judy would say, "How do I know when a teenager is lying? She's moving her mouth."

Telling the truth now and accepting the consequences for one's actions, and avoiding the more severe consequences of continued denial, requires that ability to imagine what might happen in a few days, or a couple of weeks. Mind you, a number of adult politicians don't seem to grasp this concept either.

When I was nineteen, on a beautiful day in April, it was time to study for my first year university exams scheduled to start next week. But Nikita Khrushchev had pounded his shoe on his desk in the General Assembly and Kennedy had just sent out warships to blockade the Soviet freighters and prevent them from delivering more missiles to Cuba. We were close to nuclear war. One impetuous move by a paranoid Dr. Strangelove and all would be over. I decided I'd wait this one out before committing to a week of study. What would be the point of hitting the books, unless I was studying how to survive in a post apocalypse world? A few days later Khrushchev blinked; war was averted; I headed to the library. But now that I think of it, this anecdote doesn't illustrate the late teen's limited ability to hypothesise long-term consequences, but rather his egocentricity and his unlimited capacity for rationalization.

1.3 The ability to fully appreciate human **mortality, vulnerability, and fertility.** Someone else perhaps, but not me. This is a consequence of characteristics mentioned above coupled with remnants of the special-ness experienced by a child, or the child's inexperience with cause and effect. Intellectually the adolescent knows how babies are made, how falling off a rooftop can hurt, how death is rather final. But if you live in the moment, and retain that child's sense of being special, protected, safe, then these are not consequences worth much thought. Even when the teen appears to appreciate consequences in this regard, it is often surprising how they are not **fully** appreciated. As in the fifteen-year old girl's fantasy that if she gets pregnant and has the baby, she and her seventeen-year old lover will settle in a little cottage with a white picket fence and raise the baby together. Or, as in, "If I break my leg at least I won't have to go to school for a few weeks." Or "I can't see myself living past twenty anyway." So, to get ahead of myself, don't just lecture, explain, and pull your hair out. Buy your son some condoms; take your daughter to see the family doctor about birth control; don't hesitate to apprehend the car keys; and think twice about letting your 16 year-old use the cottage, the boat or the snowmobile, with friends, unsupervised.

1.4 The ability to **plan sequentially toward a goal**. Some teenagers do develop this ability prematurely. This book is really not about that group of gifted, ambitious, clear thinking teenagers. That very ability to envision and plan toward a goal, coupled with the ambition to do it, will probably keep this teen out of trouble….unless, of course, the goal is unrealistic, the pressure to achieve too intense, or the dream is only the parent's dream.

How hard should a parent try to keep his or her child practicing piano, working on his slap shot? There is probably no clear answer to this. We know that if the ambition does not become the child's ambition, it will only lead to frustration and bitterness. But we also know that ambition can be fuelled by success. Perhaps a parent should push moderately hard for a limited time. If the child has a talent and personality suited to the pursuit, he will experience the pleasure of achievement and develop his own ambitions. If not, well, not learning to play mediocre piano or mediocre hockey is not really that important.

It is a pleasant moment for parents when the ability to imagine a future and plan toward it kicks in. "I've decided I want to be a Veterinarian." "And to become a Vet we have to what?" "Go to College?" "Right. And to get into College we have to…?" "Get my High School Credits?" "And how do we go about that?" "I guess I could go back to school. But I hate school. Maybe I could work for a year and get my credits through Adult Ed or correspondence."

It's a start. Better than, "I've decided I want to be a Rock Star." "But you don't play any instruments and you can't sing." "So?"

There was a time when the bricklayer's son became a bricklayer, the tinker's son became a tinker, and the doctor's son became a doctor. Not any longer. I remember mouthing that cliché parents' comment years ago. I said, "I don't know what the hell is wrong with him. He's doing nothing. And he's got so many more opportunities than we had at that age." "That is just the point," said his mother.

It is a modern problem. Today teenagers have endless choices, where once they had none at all. There are few absolute barriers. And whole industries and kinds of jobs and careers not imagined a few years ago. Not that they'd ever admit it, but it can be overwhelming.

Many kids go through a phase of not knowing what they want to do, so, in the meantime, while waiting for that Eureka moment, they do NOTHING. At least nothing sensible or productive. Whereupon parents exasperatedly lecture: "For God's sake do something, anything. Take a course, get a job, travel, sign up, try out. You'll find out soon enough if you like it or not." This doesn't work. In fact it can backfire. A teen will more likely take an oppositional stance to his parent's suggestions than follow them. But there are three things parents can do during this phase. 1. Wait patiently: when the brain matures those frontal lobes will

17

begin to allow the child to imagine what will happen if he spends his whole life doing nothing, and perhaps give him the confidence to try something. 2. Watch that "doing nothing" does not include becoming addicted and/or breaking the law. And 3. By practical means, not lectures, lead him or her to understand the relationship between work, money, and having things.

They treat their own money, money they earned, very differently than they treat money given to them. Just as they will treat a car they actually paid for, or paid mostly for, with money earned by themselves, very differently than they will treat your car.

There is a phase in early adolescence when you might hear from your son's lips on a bright sunny day, the birds singing, the clouds scudding across the sky, the library open, the grass begging to be cut, the words, "I'm bored. There's nothing to do." This is code for, "I retain the child's need for stimulus, entertainment, but I have not yet developed the adult's ability or confidence to initiate an activity, an exploration, an education."

You could suggest a few things he might do. Those things that involve work will be met with a groan of disbelief. And those that involve doing something you did as a teen will be met with something like, "That's so gay." (Giving the word 'gay' its third meaning in the past fifty years.)

At such moments, if you feel the need to suggest an activity, it is probably best to suggest various chores or homework. This will paradoxically spur the teen to a discourse on why that is such a bad idea, and why calling up a friend to play with is a much better idea. Actually I shouldn't be using the word 'play' here. The teen would call it 'hanging out' or simply 'hanging'.

The father, sitting across the table with both his wife and his sixteen year-old daughter, turned to me with a pained expression, and said, "I think she should have a part-time job. It would teach her some responsibility. That's what I've been telling her. But no. All she does is sit on Facebook all day." It has the ring of a lecture delivered many times.

I ask the parents about their daughter's expenses, her allowance, how much money they give her for entertainment, cell phone, I-pod, cable, special events. I add it up. I show the total to the parents. It comes perilously close to a full-time wage. Then I can't resist making my point in the following manner: I ask, "Would you consider adopting me?"

Somehow many parents seem to believe the motivation to acquire a part-time job should be intrinsic, and not simply because their teen needs to earn money to buy stuff. These same parents are surprised by the $600 bill their teen has run up on their cell phone plan. (I had written $400 bill, but just last week two parents arrived with a one-month bill of $600 their teenager had managed to accumulate.) These same teenagers, a few years later, when they are now sharing an apartment, will probably not learn that rent money should not be spent on beer, video games, or designer jeans until they have been evicted at least once.

Parents phrase the question in terms of motivation, as in, "She's just not motivated. How do I get her motivated?" Okay. We could lecture on the importance of planning for the future. We could wait for a flash of inspiration, or a muse to appear. We could hope that our child sees a ballet dancer, a doctor, a nurse, a racecar driver and says, "That's what I want to be." But in lieu of that, necessity is the strongest motivator. And parents can supply that necessity, as in, "If you don't attend school you won't have internet access." Or "If you want designer jeans, video games, the latest Nintendo or $200 for the school trip, you will have to earn it."

1.5 A full adult **conscience** or a cohesive set of values (with the exception of taking a rigid moralistic position in opposition to parental opinion).

The idealism of youth is an interesting thing: Eating meat is equated with cruelty to animals and ruining the planet. 'The church is hypocritical. Make love, not war. The teacher isn't fair. Anybody who sells drugs to children should be taken out and shot. That's just wrong. If I had a puppy I would treat her right. We will organize a massive sit-in and protest rally against a teacher rumoured to be racist. She had sex with Alicia's boyfriend. The whole world should know what a slut she is.'

Teen behaviour can seem a very confusing mixture of situational ethics, idealism, and fascism. Some of the idealism is really oppositional behaviour masquerading as idealism. The teenage girl announces she is Vegan just as Dad puts the exquisitely flavoured New York Strip on the barbecue, mesquite smoke wafting across the yard.

It is not an entirely bad thing, trying to do better than our parents. When natural oppositional behaviour leads a teen to condemn her parents' materialism, their mindless support of the status quo, their hypocrisies, their inattention to the poverty of the third world, their failed marriage, and you find her proclaiming atheism, marching against the war, volunteering at the family planning centre and telling you she intends to mate for life, (unlike you, her twice divorced father), well, it may start out as opposition but it could evolve into an admirable set of principals by which to live. Or not.

Of course a teen is as likely to foreswear your protestant work ethic, your moderation in all things, your over-long hours in the office, your attention to politics, your donations to the church, in favour of sloth and a marijuana haze. As a parent you can only hope that your teenagers, in their search for themselves, choose to

oppose your less admirable traits and ideas, and **imitate** your better ones.

But it is the nature of adolescence that in the same breath that she condemns poverty and cruelty to animals she proposes severe punishment to miscreants without recourse to due process and compassion.

Adolescence tends to be a developmental phase without subtlety or nuance. They are trying to figure this all out, using the tools of imitation, opposition, role-playing, and their own volatile feelings.

They won't rat out their friends, even a friend who has proposed breaking into your house when you are out of town. Their loyalties can be very misplaced. They are susceptible to influence, and vulnerable to extreme solutions. In North America some of the teen boys seem to take their social cues from American Prison dramas: Don't talk to the cops or the warden (parent or teacher); don't rat out a friend; exact severe punishment on those who do; expect a Nazi-like loyalty to the group or the gang.

In this state of flux they are also vulnerable to the preaching of charismatic leaders, especially those who disavow subtlety and nuance. The extremes of Islam, of Christianity, of cults and sects can appeal to a confused, frightened and disaffected teen. A sociopathic Imam or cult leader can tap into the residual anger of a teenager grieving the loss of the simplicity of childhood. And these philosophies proclaiming simple, clear divisions between good and evil, of absolute rules conferred by God, can be especially appealing to a young person developing a mental illness.

So though it looks like your teen wants nothing to do with your advice, you meat-eating, hypocritical, lapsed believer, expense account padding, armed forces supporting, SUV driving SUIT, it is still your job, through words and deed, to teach right from wrong, and all the subtleties and nuances therein. Your teen may express utter disinterest, if not disdain, for your views on such matters, but make no mistake, she is interested, if only at this moment, as a standard to oppose. In the fullness of time you may one day hear her telling her children the same things.

I have heard teens express today the same thing we said many years ago: "If I'm old enough to fight for my country, I'm old enough to drink." What does one say to that besides, "Those are the rules."?

It would be difficult to explain the full story: "Your brain is just not mature enough to allow you to take responsibility for the important decisions one must make when allowed to drink alcoholic beverages, such as when to drink such beverages, and how much to drink, and what to avoid when drinking, and when to stop drinking. Whereas it is that very immaturity that will allow you to sign up with visions of battle-field glory playing in your head, and no thought given to your own vulnerability or mortality."

1.6 The **ability to observe oneself** and one's own behaviour. When your teen answers, "Nothing." Or "Just hung out." as the answer to your question: "What did you and Kyle do all afternoon?" this actually may be about as much as he can remember of the past four hours. Of course, the joint or bong they shared might be contributing to his memory deficit.

As a writer I like to keep up to date with teen jargon. I can listen to them speak, but, curiously, when they are asked directly such questions as, "What word do you guys use today to describe something that is 'terrific' or 'lousy' or 'bad' or 'beautiful'?" they cannot tell me. Sometimes searching in their memory banks they come up with a word my generation might have used. I asked one, not unfamiliar with the subject, what he and his buddies called a marijuana cigarette these days. He looked puzzled, reflective.

Then, with a large question mark at the end of his sentence he answered, "I dunno, maybe a 'joint'?" Hey, that was my generation. Miles Davis smoked a joint now and then. Don't you guys call it a 'doob' or 'doobey' or something like that? They say these words; they express themselves. They don't listen to themselves. How else would it be possible for a 17 year old girl to use the word "like" five times in a seven word sentence? Oh my God. Oh my God.

Of course some of this might be inattention, and some might be an unwillingness to share details with an adult. So my questioning in a family assessment usually takes the form of: "So what were you doing last Friday afternoon from, say noon until nine?"

"Nothing."

"And where were you doing this 'nothing'?"

"At a friends."

"Boy or girl."

"Girl."

"Only the two of you or more?"

"Justin was there too."

"And what were the three of you doing?"

"Nothing."

"That's nine hours of nothing. You must have eaten at some time."

"Yeah, of course. In the food court, at the mall."

"So you also went to the mall."

"That's where we met up."

It may take about twenty minutes but I will learn that on this particular day of skipping school, this teen ate, listened to music, watched movies, and smoked a little marijuana. Nine hours of entertainment and gossip - the passage of time without attention paid, being aided by a little cannabis.

Your teen may be extremely self-conscious; she may be overly concerned how others see her, her haircut, her dress. But she is still not a good observer of her own behaviour.

For the boy, the teacher gave him a detention for no reason at all. He was minding his own business and Kevin hit him. He "wasn't doing nothing." These examples speak to the next point as well, but they are related.

1.7 The assumption of **personal responsibility**. This follows from the points above. If one is not observing one's own behaviour, and unable to empathize with, for example, a teacher, then it follows that it would be difficult to see the detention one received as anything but an unfair and arbitrary action.

The stories you are being told as a parent, often flavoured with outrage over the unfairness of life, about the misdeeds of others, and the arbitrary actions of teachers and coaches, the nastiness of friends, are usually missing key elements of your own child's words and behaviour. These are left out of the narrative. You might or might not be able to retrieve them before she storms off with that familiar phrase tossed over her shoulder, "You just don't understand."

What is important is to never accept the narrative presented to you as the whole truth and nothing but the truth. Though you should show interest in what your teen has to say, what he is complaining about, you don't have to accept his tale verbatim. There is almost always more to the story.

When should a parent listen to the stories of unfairness by teachers, of cruelty by friends, and take action? Well, that is the difficulty. Always believing your teen and going to bat for him or her will teach the wrong lesson. A better lesson is that the "Teacher is always right." Or perhaps, "The teacher is always to be respected, and there may be a good and constructive way for the child to deal with this conflict." Unless, of course, you have independent evidence of actual abusive behaviour on the part of a teacher, or want to participate in some general action to improve the school's resources. G. B. Shaw once commented that he learned a lot from very good teachers and very bad teachers. It was the mediocre ones who taught him little. And I think this is true. The parent who is always fighting with the teachers, the school, the principal of the school, on behalf of her child, pointing out inequities and unfairness in the teacher's methods, is usually not doing her son or daughter any favours.

The tone and tenor of the complaint against friends may help you distinguish between those times you should say, simply, "Uh huh." And those times you need to take action to stop serious bullying.

Here is the question you should ask yourself: Are the complaints about other children merely the manner in which your child is trying to engage you? As likely as not they are, especially if the child is back playing with the same guys next week. A more important sign of true bullying may be a hurt and withdrawn child who is hiding and avoiding rather than complaining.

1.8 The ability to know they don't know. Really, your teenager knows nothing. Clearly this is an exaggeration. Some teens are remarkably knowledgeable and accomplished: concert pianist, president of the debating club, editor of the school paper, star on the basketball team, planting trees and saving whales in the summer, ready and willing to discuss the merits of current foreign policy. Such successful and accomplished teens are usually not the ones in trouble, save for the odd bout of anxiety when they have trouble living up to their own and their parents' high expectations.

But most teens, and certainly most of the ones in trouble, know nothing. Well, as they will tell you, they do know lots of stuff, though determining what that "stuff" is can be a daunting task. I suspect most of it falls in the realm of pop culture (the hottest bands, lead singers, Rap lyrics, fashion), and local peer gossip.

The point of my exaggeration (Your teenager knows nothing) is to suggest that we vastly overestimate their knowledge of the world in which we really live. They are, potentially, exposed to far more information than previous generations. In theory they can watch news channels 24/7, The Discovery Channel, and mini-series and features that cover historical events with some accuracy. They can surf the Internet for information on any subject imaginable. But they don't watch the former, and the latter is just another form of entertainment.

I had the opportunity to attend a couple of movies about J. F. Kennedy and then Harry Truman with two adolescents, and then question them afterwards about the historical events and context of the films. They might as well have been watching Star Wars. And just as the intricacies of the relationship between the Federation and the Rebels and the Jedi might remain a mystery to them (as it is to me) as they watch the love story, the fighting, the weird creatures, and the special effects, so too did the politics and historical context of Kennedy's and Truman's presidencies remain a complete mystery. It was just entertainment, in one ear and out the other, as my grandmother would say.

Most teens, with exceptions of course, are also not curious. When I ask how their MP3 player works, how on earth do they get music from that little box of electronics, they usually answer with incredulity, "You push the 'on' button, stupid." Sometimes the "stupid" is said, sometimes implied by the inflection. When asked what keeps a plane in the sky, very few have a clue. And most of those who don't know are also not curious.

"How do you expect me to know that?" they say. "It's not important in my life."

"I don't expect you to know," I tell them. "But do you ever wonder about it?"

Despite plaintive queries of, "Why Not?" and "I'm not a kid, you know." your adolescent has few skills, little knowledge, and very little confidence. Unfortunately, he cannot know and appreciate this (see point one) and thus you must determine, assess his level of knowledge, skill, competence, and confidence, from his or her behaviour.

We would like our teens to make good choices, responsible decisions. And each time they do this, growth occurs. But they may not have the knowledge to make those decisions and choices. They protest that they have; but they may not. Their behaviour will tell you what they really know and don't know, but it is best to assume they don't have the wisdom or knowledge to handle very much until they prove to you they can.

2. Performance

2.1 Your teenager is seeking an independent identity, trying to find and define himself or herself **apart from you**. The only tools your teenager has to accomplish this are **Opposition** and **Imitation**. This is why, on one hand, she will say she "is expressing herself" while you observe her actually mimicking the dress and behaviour of her friends and/or a current pop star, and on the other hand, opposing your ideas and instructions almost as a reflex action.

This process of imitating and opposing will happen. You can hope it takes a benign, if sometimes irritating course. Perhaps the vehement opposition will actually be pleasing, as in a definite NO to drugs. And the imitation might be of your better traits and opinions.

But it is just as likely that your opposition to marijuana will provoke endless arguments about the spiritual yet harmless qualities of weed, and that she will blindly copy the sexually provocative clothing of a rock star. Or worse. He will imitate the dress and language and ethics portrayed in a crime show. She will imitate the dress and manner of a wasted heroin addict.

The teenager with growing skills and competencies (in sports, music, academics, clubs, part-time jobs, etc.) will likely oppose and imitate in a relatively safe and moderate fashion.

Opposition to you and your ways will come in the form of hair shape and colour, terrible noise he calls music, ripped jeans, untied shoelaces, school tartan rolled up a couple of inches, pants a few sizes too big, six earrings when one would suffice. These are all necessary components of defining himself or herself as "not you".

But if not you, who? Maybe Avril Lavigne, Hannah Montana, Miley Cyrus, the cool dudes in grade 12, or maybe sunken eyed heroin addicts or baggy panted, bling-wearing low level drug dealers.

The teenager who is not developing skills and competencies is more likely to oppose you vehemently and imitate more outrageous forms of dress and behaviour. The squarest mother and father I ever met from middle-class suburbia, he a bookkeeper, she the mayor of a small town: their daughter became the living canvas for a tattoo artist. The police chief's son leads the cops of a neighbouring town on a high-speed chase. The teacher's son drops out of school.

I did my best to not overtly push my children toward university, but the writing was on the wall. They were members of a mostly academic and professional extended family. My daughter did not attend university. But many years later she emailed me the following: "Got a promotion and a raise. My salary is now six figures, and I did it without going to university like you wanted me to." So that push-pull of wanting to please and oppose at the same time still lingers. She found her own way, as they all must. And Dad is very proud of her.

A teenager experiencing success in at least one sphere of his or her life (home, school, sports, music, clubs, church, etc.) is at lower risk than the kid failing at everything. That is the child, the one not fitting in, not succeeding, who is likely to adopt the most outrageous positions of opposition and imitation.

What on earth is the appeal of Goth, you ask? But that is the very point. You put on your power suit, apply subtle makeup, the right pair of shoes, and carry your briefcase to your office job. She wears black; she colours her hair black; she paints dark circles around her eyes, inserts metal in her lip, her nose, her ear, and God help us, her tongue. It is as far away as possible from the way you dress and the way you would like her to dress. And that is the point of it. Though she won't be able to see that for a good 10 years. Right now she is defining herself as **anything but you** and imitating something from a rock video or a vampire movie. If there are a few Goths at her school, it will also provide some membership, some belonging. Though you would much prefer she play on the softball or soccer team.

So make sure your teen experiences success, and develops some competencies in some sphere of his or her life. If not academics, then sports. If not sports, then music, if not music then cadets, or photography, riding horses, looking after pets, fixing things, babysitting, working part-time.

But the teen's sense of being an independent being, a formed and functioning creation, a creature of substance, of control, of opinion, of confidence as they walk among their peers, is a fragile thing.

This is why, when you ask a simple question, you get shut down.

Your son comes through the door. You ask, benignly, simply, nicely, "How was your day at school today?"

He responds with snarl, with attitude, "The usual crap." And heads off somewhere. You can also hear, in his voice, a tacit, "None of your business."

You thought you were displaying appropriate interest as a parent, asking a simple, uncluttered social and pedagogical question. But what he heard was, "Father once again intruding on my fragile sense of self, challenging my independence." Down periscope.

Maybe he will talk with you later.

At a seminar I attended I heard a psychologist talk about how his son, when he drove him to a school dance, insisted that he be dropped off a block away from the school, and then picked up later that evening at the same spot. He was using that as an example of how, at that age, teens want nothing to do with their parents, that their parents' attitudes and opinions are of no interest to them, that the companionship and opinions of their peers are all that mattered to them. I think he was suggesting that these kids were now too old for family therapy.

He was wrong, of course. Sure, kids go through a stage of wanting to distance themselves from their parents when they are around their peers. They do not want the two worlds to collide. But this is not because the parents' attitudes and opinions are not important to them. Au contraire. It is the fact the parents' opinions and reactions are important to them that they crave some separation.

The boy is going to a school dance. He has been rehearsing in his mind for some time how to behave, where to stand, how to walk, how to talk, how to ask a girl to dance. He wants to be a man among men. He has showered long and shaved carefully. He has dressed in just the right balance of formal and informal. He has gelled his hair. He is about to engage in a courtship ritual. He must not be too enthusiastic. He must be cool. He must not allow his insecurity to show. He is entering into a role and he is not well practiced. He knows he may stumble, or overplay his coolness. He does not want his father to observe this very unpolished   . performance. He does not want to appear foolish or phoney in his father's eyes. He would never admit it, but his father's opinion of him is very important. He is merely saying, "Please, let me practice my cool dude personae and my courtship ritual in private."

Many years ago, a few days before Christmas, my brother and I arrived at our older sister's house, to visit with our mother. We arrived with our girlfriends just as a big winter storm swept through the town. We had plans to visit with friends later that evening but the storm locked us in. The roads were impassable.

After dinner the four of us sat on the floor of the living room listening to music. Someone rolled a joint and passed it around. Our mother was in the kitchen talking with our sister. We were doing the joint ritual thing on the living room floor, holding it daintily between index finger and thumb, pointing up about 45 degrees, sucking and sucking and sucking with those quick inhales, and then holding and holding, and then letting out slowly with pursed lips saying, "Tha's good shit, man." and then passing carefully to the left, when our mother walked in. It was our sister's house. We didn't live at home anymore. Our mother stood there looking down on us for a good long beat. And then she said, "If you only knew how silly you look." She turned and went back to the kitchen to resume her conversation with our sister and drink her instant coffee with condensed milk.

It is not an oddity that I remember this moment, for how we appear to our parents during this phase of life is at least as important as how we appear to our peers and ourselves. We are just not sure how to reconcile the two.

2.2 Teens crave membership and acceptance. Ideally this will come through skills and productive activities and success: Membership in Mr. B's Grade 8 class, halfback on the soccer team, flute player in the band, reporter on the school paper, the chess club, the science club, cadets. All too often membership can mean a loose association of teens who "hang out" together. They hang at the mall, or in someone's basement, listening to music, watching movies. They are not developing skills, and membership and acceptance can be a fickle thing, depending on shared dislikes, shared prejudices, shared fears and temporary alliances. A little purposeless "hanging out" may be good; a lot is always bad. The alliances break; the group gets bored and seeks excitement; sexual tension erupts into soap opera triangles, no skills are developed; self-esteem suffers; alcohol and drugs beckon.

The teenager who is not developing any skills and competencies may be attracted to **groups defined by a prejudice, a shared fear, or gangs and cults**. When a teen has no skills and competencies and a powerful need to oppose and imitate and belong, the gang offers a ready-made way of opposing parents, teachers, authority, and of imitating a style abhorrent to parents, teachers, authorities, while at the same time maintaining the illusion of the comfort and safety of a family. And, possibly, the development of a skill set and competencies we would rather them not have. Of course if the child's own family is in disarray, an alternative family is quite appealing.

The teen has left childhood behind. He is beginning to see the inequities in the world. He has lost the omnipotence of a child. But he has not developed any sense of competence to replace this. He has anger. He has love. He has fear. How should he direct these? The gang, the cult, they give him ready answers and return his sense of omnipotence; he can be valued without having skills; he can oppose his parents and still have a family; he can regain the black and white world of childhood; he has a place to direct his anger. He can acquire a mentor, a father figure. And none of this requires him to think as an adult or assume any personal responsibility.

Your teen needs to belong to something, to be a member of some group. Try to make it the baseball team and your family. He needs to develop competencies. Try to make it playing the violin,

33

or changing a tire, or serving coffee, or babysitting, not assembling a fertilizer bomb, loading a weapon, or being the spotter for a drug deal.

2.3 It is your teenager's job to test boundaries, that is, to discover by his or her own behaviour what is acceptable and permitted, safe or unsafe, and with or without serious consequences. They do have to find out some things for themselves. It is your job as parent to decide when to smile, grimace, cross your fingers and roll your eyes, and when to say **STOP**. Remember that chimp who insisted on joining the tribe across the river? Even though he suffered beatings and starvation, he did manage to enrich the gene pool. So it is not the actual testing of boundaries that is bad necessarily; that is a part of adolescence. The testing can be safe or unsafe, innocuous or important. Skipping school can be a "Ferris Bueller's Day Off" or it can threaten continued attendance at school and future vocations. It may be, in fact, the adolescent drive to test boundaries that ultimately results in social and technological progress. So we don't want to quell it altogether.

But not every teen is an Edison or a James Meredith. Most of the time this testing of boundaries will not advance the human condition. So watch carefully, and figure out when you need to say, "**STOP**". On the other hand, if your teen does not test any boundaries whatsoever, and is always fully compliant and obedient, this could foreshadow more serious problems to come.

Some time ago we rented a large space below us to a woman who wanted to conduct art classes. The space opened up onto a large patio with garden and birdbath. One night she allowed her teenage daughter to celebrate a birthday in the space, unsupervised. Of course text messages went out, the crowd swelled. Fifteen, sixteen year-olds poured out onto the

34

patio. The music got louder. A bong appeared. Beer, wine, and cheap liquor. Another bong appeared, or maybe it was what they call a bucket. They were getting stoned and drunk. We phoned the mother of the girl and suggested she come over and supervise. She agreed, but said it would take some time to get there.

The party got louder. More teens arrived. And then, as I watched from the floor above, one boy, unsteady on his feet, unzipped his fly and urinated in the birdbath. My birdbath.

It was time to take action. There is a deck overlooking this backyard, with stairs going down to it. I stood on the deck and summoned up my best School Principal Voice, and told them they had fifteen minutes to clean up and clear out before the police arrived.

They stopped in their tracks. They looked up at me. One boy actually said, "Yes sir. Sorry sir." The music ceased. They went about cleaning up and exiting as I stood with arms crossed on the deck above them. I went back to enjoy the quiet of my living room and sip a glass of wine.

And then I felt a spasm of guilt. Really, these were nice kids, polite kids, good kids. And God knows they were doing nothing that I hadn't done at that age.

But then I thought, no. They had done their job, and I had done my job. They were pushing the limits, testing the boundaries, challenging the rules, and I had stood up as a surrogate parent and said, "Stop." And they had stopped. All was right with the world.

2.4 They want you to keep them safe, deep in their hearts, despite their behaviour, their opposition, their willingness to sneak out of the house and engage in relationships with unsavoury and even dangerous people. Though they may fight you on it every step of the way **they often want you to say "NO"**.

They want you to intervene and stop them from engaging in unsafe behaviour. When a teenager pushes boundaries to unsafe and harmful levels he or she often does so in clear view, or in a manner easily discovered. That is, he or she is sending you a message that it is time to say **STOP**. Although, of course, they won't thank you when you do.

This is a tricky area. Your job as a parent is to **watch their behaviour, rather than listen to their words**. She may protest vehemently that she wants to do something, that she must do something. You say "NO". She continues to protest. She may retreat in a sulk and slam a bedroom door. And though she may protest that you have ruined her life, her sulk passes quickly, her anxiety drops. She may even become pleasant. Providing of course, that seeing her withdraw from you, seeing her unhappiness, you have **not** pursued her into her bedroom to "have a talk" and assuage your guilt.

In one of Garrison Keillor's clever monologues he illustrates this with wonderful insight. The parents are away for the weekend. The teenage boy has the house to himself. He allows a gathering to occur. The party grows. At times during the evening he thinks he should intervene, rationalizes that he will have time in the morning to clean up the broken vase, re-hang the door, get rid of the bottles, concoct an excuse. He has a beer, relaxes. His peers have taken over the whole house; the music plays loudly; fluids have been spilled on the living room carpet. He feels he should do something. He has another beer. He can rent a carpet cleaner in the morning. The party has spilled outside; the music is louder. It is past midnight now. He has another beer. Then through the living room window he sees the bubble lights, the rotating red and blue lights of a couple of police cars arriving at the house. And he feels ......
relieved.

36

In sessions with families, when I am holding the parents' attention, and telling them something like, "Your kid needs you to be clear about her curfew. Exactly by what time must she be home on Friday and Saturday? You are the parents. It's your decision". – more than once the watching 15 year-old has said to her parents, "I could have told you that."

I ask a teen in a family session what time her curfew is on Saturday night. She asks if I want to know the real one or the other one. I ask her to explain this. She says, "Well, they tell me I'm supposed to be home by eleven, but they don't get really mad unless it's after one."

Which leads naturally to the following advice: Consider there to be three levels of adolescent misdeeds. The first is a behaviour that will eventually self-correct, is not dangerous or life altering. For this category you need but smile inwardly, roll your eyes, reassure yourself that this will pass. The second category requires a little reminder, corrective advice, some motherly nagging. You must do your duty but not expect any dramatic change in behaviour. Perhaps this would include brushing of teeth, wet towel dropped on the bathroom floor, large sneakers left in the kitchen, homework procrastination, messy bedroom. But there is a third category of behaviours you have decided cannot be tolerated in your family. If this is true, then the boundary must be defined carefully and specifically (adolescents are all good lawyers), and the consequences spelled out in detail. And then you must follow through with the consequences, without hesitation, without argument, without guilt and unnecessary explanation. The consequence should happen now (not "the next time you're invited to a party"), and be of short duration. The former follows simple behavioural principals: you want the misdeed and the consequence to be clearly linked in your child's memory. The second piece of advice accepts the short attention span of youth, the manner in which teens live in the moment. If the grounding, the taking away

37

of the computer, or X-Box, or the car keys, is of too long a duration or for an unspecified duration, it is, in the teen's mind, 'forever', and thus might as well be ignored. But if it is for a short duration, say a week, maybe two weeks, then the teen can imagine the return of the privilege upon his good behaviour.

It is not unusual to talk with a parent who has set a boundary, whose teen has broken that boundary or rule, and then been, for example, grounded for a week. The teen stays home for the week, locked off the Internet, cell phone removed. She attends school, comes home. But the parent is still unhappy with the teen, because the teen is unhappy with her punishment, and is still sulky and arguing.

The rule has been established. The rule has been broken. A consequence has been applied successfully. Excellent parenting. Expecting the child to show appreciation for this is silly. That appreciation won't arrive for ten years or so. The attitude display, the sulkiness, belongs in the first category of misbehaviour and should be ignored. In fact, if you don't ignore it, and allow the teen to re-engage you over the issues at hand, you have just undermined your own effective parenting.

2.5 Sometimes they're grown up, sometimes they're not.

There is a phase in late teens and early twenties that has been called the "novice phase of adulthood." We could also call it "post-adolescence". During these years a parent can never be sure if he is facing a child, an adolescent, or a young adult, or an adolescent trying out adult behaviours, or a twenty-something displaying remnants of adolescent thinking.

The father is on the top steps of a 12-foot ladder trying to detach the housing of a fluorescent light. The gangling, strong, athletic 19-year old comes by. He says, "I can do that for you. Lemme do it."

The father says, "Are you sure you know how?"

The boy answers, "Course I know how. I'm not stupid."

The father is thinking, "Ah, the novice phase of adulthood. He wants to be helpful. He wants to demonstrate his competence. How delightful. He may even be showing some empathy for a man too old to be standing on the top rung of a 12 foot stepladder."

The father climbs down. The boy climbs up. The boy grasps the housing in his strong hands. Within seconds there comes the sound of plastic and glass breaking, and bits falling to the floor.

The boy climbs down the ladder. He says, "Damn thing was broken already. You can probably get a new one for ten bucks at Home Depot. I'm outa here."

"Ah," sighs the father. Back to adolescence: Not my fault; not my responsibility; not my problem; and certainly not my money.

2.6 To ask the question "Why?" in regard to much adolescent behaviour is often fruitless. Of course the usual phrase that roles from a parent's tongue is, "What on earth were you thinking?" This question implies that there might be a logical and adult kind of motivation behind the behaviour.

But outrageous adolescent behaviour often occurs simply because **it is possible**. He is testing boundaries. She is finding out what is possible and what is not. Thus, if the opportunity arises to stay up all night and drink toxic amounts of Vodka she might do it simply because it is possible to do it. No one at that moment is saying "No." If the opportunity arises to find out just how fast a corner can be taken before rolling Mom's car, he might, with encouragement from friends, avail himself of said opportunity.

Unfortunately, the only way to find that particular limit is to actually roll the car.

If the opportunity to shoplift arises, with encouragement from friends, she might try it, to see what it's like, to see what it feels like, if it's possible.

After the phone call to pick up the intoxicated daughter, or call a wrecking company for the car, or come down to the Mall Security Office, we might find ourselves asking, "What on earth got into you?" and "What were you thinking?" But we won't get a satisfying answer to this question.

It is more useful to ask, "Did you learn anything?"

And to simply understand that this particular adolescent is not quite ready for this much freedom. The Vodka drinker is not ready for unsupervised over-nights. The car roller should not have unsupervised access to his mother's car again until he has paid for the damage, taken driving lessons, and demonstrated a higher level of responsible behaviour. Shoplifting may bring about its own consequences but certainly it would imply that this teenager is not ready for so much unsupervised hanging-out at the mall.

Parents, in frustration and bewilderment, lecture their adolescents, reason with them, and try to pound sense into their heads. In family counselling sessions they turn to me and say, "She's got to understand that (she needs an education - he'll end up flipping burgers if he drops out of school - he'll end up in jail if he - she'll ruin her health if she….)" and I always say, "No, you and I need to understand that ….she can't yet understand it. Her brain isn't there yet, or at least her need to be oppositional overwhelms any ability she might have to listen to good advice and logic and plan sequentially toward a goal. We need to understand what he or she needs to do, or stop doing, and then we, meaning you, the parents, need to act accordingly." So when the boy is seventeen and wants to drop out of school, it is not a question of pointing out over and over again the importance of an education, but rather stating the obvious fact of life that the boy's choices are to either attend school and receive free room and board and internet access in this house, or find a job and pay for his room and board and internet access here or somewhere else.

2.7 A language all their own. Teens develop a jargon, a vocabulary of expressions du jour, that may have come to them from movies, television, the internet, and which might have originated in the streets of Baltimore, Los Angeles, Liverpool or New York. Generally, these are ways of expressing what is felt to be either bad or good in a manner foreign to their parents. The simplest being, of course, to assign a given word a meaning opposite to the one understood by a parent. So 'bad' might mean 'good'. 'Sick' replaces 'sweet'. But there is another creative way they use language that is more in keeping with George Orwell or the old Soviet Union, or Madison Avenue. Words can be given their own definitions. They can be vehicles for obfuscation and avoidance. And if we're not on our toes we miss it. Like going to war to achieve peace. Like the Peoples Democratic Republic of China. Like all pigs are created equal, but some are more equal than others. Like low fat donuts and no payment required for 18 months, just a small administrative fee.

"Mostly" and "Pretty much" are good ones. "Mostly" when applied to the question, "Have you done your homework?" can mean anything from, "It crossed my mind fleetingly an hour ago" to "I'm a third of the way through it."

"Pretty much", as an answer to the question, "Have you stopped smoking marijuana?" can mean "I'm down to one joint a day." Or when applied to the question, "Did you pass all your courses?" can mean anything from one out of five to three out of five. I suspect had the teen in question passed four out of five the answer would have been simply, "Sure" or "Of course." This would be a lie, but only because he did not speak aloud, and you did not hear, the **qualifier**.

A tacit qualifier is often required to understand teen speak. In this case, the spoken, "Sure" was probably followed by an unspoken, "I didn't need that fifth course anyway" or "The geography teacher was lousy so that course doesn't count."

"Jonny, did you pass all your courses?"

"Sure. Of Course." ("Geography was elective so it doesn't count.")

"Have you really quit smoking marijuana?"

"Totally." ("Except the times someone gives me a joint, at a party or someplace.")

"So you didn't get any detentions this semester?"

"No. None." (The two in February don't count because it wasn't my fault.")

And speaking of lying, my very own favourite teen phrase is: "I swear to God." This seems to mean, as far as I can tell, something like this: "Usually I bullshit a little, tell half truths, dissemble somewhat, but this time I have told you a total and complete lie."

2.8 Whatever you fear or worry that your teenager is doing – he is probably doing it. Trust your intuition. Thus when you find yourself saying, "He tells me when he's hanging out with Kyle, they're just talking and listening to music, but I worry that he may be smoking marijuana." He probably is.

And when you find yourself saying, "He says he and Kyle just smoke weed when they hang out, but I have a feeling they might be experimenting with Ecstasy or this Crystal Meth stuff." They probably are.

Perhaps there are times when a parent's anxieties and fantasies far out-strip their adolescent's actual possibilities and proclivities, but usually a parent's anxieties are based on some kind of subtle data: the few hours not accounted for, the somewhat glazed look in the child's eyes, the money missing you might have miscounted, the stealthy trip from back door to bedroom without pausing to see what you are watching on television, the heavy looking backpack going out the front door....

So if your intuition is telling you something is amiss, it probably is. You should look into it. As mentioned before, he probably wants you (deep in his heart) to find out anyway, and to intervene. Don't hesitate to invade his or her privacy. This is not an adult renting a condo from you. This is your child living in your house.

The risk, of course, is the wrongly accused adolescent. There is no indignation like the wrongly accused adolescent's indignation. (Although there are times the rightly accused adolescent can put on a display of indignation almost as dramatic) Not to worry though. If it happens that you find you were wrong, simply do the adult thing and apologize.

2.9 What the teenager says to you often needs to be decoded. If you respond to the surface message you are likely to get stuck in a frustrating argument. The teenager lives in the moment and must, as a developmental task, be constantly negotiating the parameters of the relationship he or she has with parents. Those parameters are **boundaries, responsibility, control, power, worth, and competence**. So often the ostensible, overt question or statement is not as important as the **underlying negotiation**. In fact the surface statement or argument, or apparent subject, may not have any importance whatsoever. **It is the underlying negotiation that is important, that will determine what will happen next.** The ostensible subject may be simply a vehicle used for the other, more important negotiation. This may be, simply, a negotiation, here and now, over who is in control, or who is responsible, or who has power, or who has worth, value, and competence. And where are the real fences and boundaries?

"There's nothing to do and I'm bored" really means, "I do not yet have the confidence and skill to initiate an activity. I suspect you are responsible to entertain me like you used to."

"Algebra is stupid. I'll never use it" really means, "I don't understand it. It sounds like work. I am afraid to try because I might fail. I want to feel competent but I don't feel competent."

"I don't know anything about ......it's of no interest to me." Really means "I don't understand because I know very little and I don't want to be aware of how much I don't know and don't understand, because that is very frightening."

"Can I grow marijuana in the back yard this summer?" really means, "I'm at loose ends, unsure of myself, and need to engage a parent in an oppositional struggle. I need to negotiate boundaries. I need to provoke you into saying something I can oppose."

And, "Is it okay if Kailyn and me hitchhike to Toronto to attend the M&M concert, stay over with Kailyn's cousin's boyfriend, and get a ride back home on Sunday?" really means, "Is there anyone here who loves me enough to say NO and keep me safe?"

Some sniffles and a rant about how life sucks, even ending with a statement such as, "I might as well be dead." can simply mean, "Does anybody out there love me."

2.10 It may be harder today. Socrates and every generation of parents since have complained about the behaviour and attitudes of adolescents. But there are differences now, and they have increased dramatically in the last twenty years.

Generally, there is more money available; but even when the parents' incomes are small, the teens' expectations may be Orange County. I am always astonished to see, in many low-income families, that it has become the right of a 13 year-old girl to have the latest cell phone. The child is dressed in designer labels, expensive shoes, carefully applied expensive make-up, I-POD in hand while the mother clearly shops for herself at Value Village.

All right, you do not want your child to appear disadvantaged, to feel unloved. But this is simply wrong and explains without need for more data why this child speaks and behaves in such an entitled fashion and is currently on suspension for saying nasty things to a teacher.

Though most fathers are fond of saying, "When I was your age....." we actually forget how different it was, how little we had and were given as children, how we caught the bus or walked to get somewhere, how we had to sit around bored while our parents entertained adult friends.

Circumstances dealt a severe blow to our childhood sense of entitlement as we navigated adolescence. We did ride bicycles to school. A 10-cent balsam glider was a special treat. We saved money from berry picking in the summer to send away for a Radio Shack kit. We built speakers from a design in Popular Mechanics. We acquired part-time jobs as fast as we could because we knew that was the only way we were going to get those 45's and LP's and sports equipment we coveted. Okay. That was many years ago. This current generation of parents may remember saving allowance money to buy a CD, working in the summer to pay for a school trip, getting a CD player for Christmas,

But now we are all part of the new age, driving our SUV's to Boston Pizza and settling in for a night in front of the high definition big screen TV with surround sound. And every kid has a cell phone in his pocket, ear buds in his ears, Nintendo in hand, while coveting the new I PAD.

Adolescent expectations regarding food, toys, clothing, communication devices, and transportation are much higher than even a generation ago. Their expectations of privilege and freedom are higher. Their sense of entitlement is greater. They can remain financially and emotionally dependent on their parents for much longer.

There are increasing numbers of ways to get in trouble in this modern world. Teens are exposed to more information, of a sort, than previous generations. And, finally, often overlooked but probably of most importance, **they can now communicate with one another interminably (as well as with con artists, hucksters, predators, and charismatic paranoids).**

This latter reality is very new. And it means that during a phase of life in which adolescents are exploring, for themselves, the great questions of social intercourse, social contract, intimacy, belonging, membership, codes of conduct, identity, loyalty, ambition, right and wrong, forgiveness, redemption and retribution, they are far more likely, than previous generations, to be doing it among themselves, away from the eyes and ears and input of parents or other mature, caring, and experienced people.

The problems that arise from this can range from a group of teens independently dreaming up a bit of drama (based on a song, a movie, a TV show, a chat room, a video game) to teach an errant member of the group a lesson, all the way to concocting a delusional worldview and acting upon it.

My father had to worry we might be too influenced by Timothy Leary. I had to worry my son might be too influenced by Madison Avenue. Today parents must worry their teens will be too influenced by each other, and by their own interpretations of the lessons taught by first-person shooter video games, Facebook slander, impulsive twitters, misogynist Rap music, MSN gossip, satanic websites, self-mutilation websites, and texting confessions of love, sex, and betrayal. And, of course, some parents need to worry their daughter is too influenced by the charming sexual predator posing as a 15 year old she has met on an Internet chat room.

The sixteen year-old boy has returned home after a few weeks on the street and in the shelters. He is abiding by the house rules for now. He is not using drugs. He has applied for a job. He wants to work in the summer and go back to school in the fall. The parents, finally, have applied a little tough love. They are clear this time: if he breaks his probation order they will breach him. If they catch him stealing and using drugs again they will throw him out. He is cool with this. But one problem remains: He is sexually active with a fifteen-year-old girl and he is not using condoms.

I had met with the mother and father once before when the boy was out of the house and suggested they bring him in when he returned home. Now he is home and mostly behaving himself, except for the risk of getting a fifteen year-old pregnant. As with many teens he harbours a fantasy of a happy little arrangement with his girlfriend and a little baby in a little house. We attempt to engage this boy about sex, pregnancy, the reality of parenthood, and STD's. Sprawled in his chair, ball cap on backwards, baggy pants above big sneakers, a world-weary expression on his face, he tells us, "I never talk about sex with old people."

They now have the opportunity to develop codes of conduct, ideas about themselves and their relationship to the rest of the world, among themselves, without reference to adults, and adult institutions and history - at least without reference to those adults and adult institutions which we would want to have influence on our teens.

Unfortunately, besides each other, they also take their cues from those adults and adult controlled industries which have, as their sole purpose, the exploitation of this newly affluent demographic.

A few years ago this adolescent-to-adolescent communication could happen only during limited unsupervised time together, and carefully allotted telephone time. Today, with their own cell phones, text messaging, and access to MSN and the Internet, teenagers can, and sometimes do, talk to one another around the clock.

Asking how many hours the teen spends on video games, MSN or Facebook, on the cell phone texting, has become a standard question in any psychiatric and family assessment. Of course the teen cannot tell you the answers to these questions with any accuracy (see point above about not being good observers of their own behaviour) so the full measure must be determined by taking the teen and her parents through an hour-by-hour day, and thus finding "not much" really means ten hours per day, complete with cell phone left on under the pillow after midnight in case a text message comes in.

So it has become standard advice to all parents: **monitor this, and insist on more time spent in supervised, skill building, confidence building activities, and less time in unsupervised random discourse with peers.**

The shy teen, the avoidant teen, the anxious teen, and the teen suffering an actual Anxiety Disorder now have a place to hide. And that place can become an addiction. The boy drops out of school, sleeps during the day, gets up sometime in the afternoon and begins playing video games.

Apart from occasional foraging in the refrigerator he plays until he falls asleep about four or five in the morning. Some of these games offer an illusion of community, talking with other players online. Perhaps before, at school, he suffered anxiety. He may even have suffered feelings that others watched and judged him. But now he is comfortable, lost in his games. With headphones on he talks with other gamers. Modern technology has created a place this teen can hide from the anxiety-provoking real world, complete with an illusion of community, some stimulation, (an awful lot of a certain kind of stimulation), a particular skill development, and a growing addiction. There are some boys who will parlay this addiction into an actual career but for most it needs to be monitored and limited. A stand-up comic, making light of this new problem, mimicked such a gamer emerging into the sunlight about age 35 and saying, "What? Was I supposed to mate or something?"

The girl, too anxious or phobic or troubled to engage in the real world with her peers, may spend her days in the virtual reality of SIMS or hours texting inane messages back and forth with her "friends". Inevitably someone's feelings are hurt by a thoughtless message; the teen has a "meltdown" at home, which, in the parents' eyes, arrives unexpectedly, and unprovoked.

It is pleasant to fantasize rolling back the clock, stopping some inventions from ever happening. Did we really need computer war games for teenage boys? Do teenage girls really need to be connected with their peers 24/7?

As with all technological advances no one could accurately predict how they would be developed, sold and used in the real world. The automobile was first thought to be a plaything for the very rich. It was thought the telephone, Alexander Graham Bell's invention, might at least be useful in the case of emergencies.

I experienced a few years of annoyance when, the plane having landed at the airport and taxied to a stop, dozens of passengers would find it necessary to bring out their cell phones to tell someone in the arrivals lounge that they had arrived, that the plane had landed. I didn't hear this on my most recent trip. I suspect they are now all texting the message to their waiting families and friends, whom I would have thought were capable of reading flight information on the flat screen monitors in front of them.

I think I understood how much the world had changed some years ago when we set up a tent in the wilderness of a remote state park and, walking to fetch some water, I came across a field where at both ends fellow campers were talking into cell phones saying, "Can you hear me now? Is the signal clear?"

As much as we would like, we cannot undo technological advances. How it will all evolve we have yet to see. We probably can't keep our boys from playing some violent video games, prevent our daughters from having cell phones, shut down all of You Tube, Facebook, twitter, MSN, get rid of Porn sites, eliminate all stupid and false information from the world wide web. But in our homes, when our kids are between the ages of one and nineteen, **we need to monitor, limit, and, sometimes, put a stop to all of the above.** At the very least we need to try to help them understand the implications of posting their thoughts, conversations, opinions and photos on the internet.

2.11 By temperament some adolescents are easy to raise and others more difficult. Some respond to a look of disappointment on mother's face. Others require the loss of the cell phone, loss of MSN, and grounding, before they relent.

It is always wise to remember, when confronting stubbornness, passivity, anxiety, and rising temper in a teen, the acorn does not fall far from the tree. It is often the parent and teen with very similar temperaments who butt heads. The stubborn, argumentative teen can always get a rise out of a stubborn, argumentative adult.

Sometimes they are too like us. Sometimes they are too unlike us. When they are too like ourselves we tend to over-identify, to project too much of ourselves into our teens. The father dreamt of playing professional hockey as a boy, but around age 16 he discovered girls and weed and beer. Now he goes to his son's games to encourage, to cheer. But the 16 year-old son has discovered girls and weed and beer and he's lazy on the ice. This is infuriating to the father.

The mother says, "She's manipulating. She knows what she's doing. She's just being nasty." Or "He's exactly like his father."

When they are too much like ourselves we tend to relive our own struggles and failures through their lives. We empathize. Sometimes we empathize too much, become over protective, over solicitous, over involved. Sometimes in the office it is difficult to tell if the Anxiety resides in the child, or the parent, or both.

When they are too unlike ourselves we tend to be astonished, and then rendered impotent by their behaviour. "I would never have dreamt of saying something like that to my father." Not being able to empathize with the behaviour of this child we are at risk of ascribing perverse motivation to it, to see it as a character flaw that is very annoying. The rudeness, the disrespect, the lying, the disobedience.

51

The hard working ambitious father hates to see, what he describes as "laziness", in his son. Lack of motivation. "He just doesn't care about his future."

But each kid is different. And he or she is not you. He may be more or less like you, but he is not you. But he is you, you say. He walks like you. He laughs like you. But then again you were never rude to teachers. So he is not enough like you.

Ahh. It is very confusing. We love them, identify with them, empathize with them, feel protective, disappointed, hurt, angry.

This may be why, fairy tales aside, the stepparent almost always has a better perspective. He or she may be fond of the child, may even love the child, but they don't over identify. They more easily see the teen in question as a separate being with his or her own developing temperament, skills, competencies, charms, failings and flaws.

What possible advice could one pull from this complexity? Maybe it is simply to try to remember that though the child is yours, carries your genes (or not) they have their own temperaments, they may be more or less impulsive than you were, more or less inhibited than you were, more or less frightened than you were, more or less ambitious than you were, more or less outgoing than you were, more or less risk taking than you were, more or less enthralled by authority than you were. And thus you might need different strategies to keep them safe and guide them to successful adulthood.

2.12 When your teen hits adolescence he is no longer "your child". His or her very need to individuate, to separate emotionally, dictates that those moments of quiet heart-to-heart talks, those moments of warm shared experience may be rare. Cherish them when they occur. Don't expect them. Your job now is to be his MOTHER or FATHER when warranted, when needed, when circumstances demand it, when his behaviour demands it, when he wants it, but much of the time to be a **watchful, sane, responsible, parsimonious over-seer.**

A paradox may arise between a parent and a teen. The more dependent a 16 year-old boy is on his parents, the more emotionally bonded to his mother, the more often he may need to be surly and defiant, to push his mother away with attitude and nasty language. This can play out in an unhealthy manner: The boy pushes mom away. She tries harder to reach out to him. She looks hurt that he has pushed her away. He feels bad that she looks hurt. He feels guilt, burdened by his mother's sadness, and this turns to anger. His emotions are in turmoil: he wants his mom; he wants to be a man. He must fight against his child-like wish to be enfolded in his mother's arms. He pushes her away with more vitriol, defiance, and rude language.

The mother complains that her 17 year-old boy is disrespectful, disobedient, does nothing to help, displays no gratitude. She feels she has no power with him, no authority. He does not love her.

But he is still living at home. Still asking her for money. He is still emotionally and financially dependent on his mother. This is the paradox. The very boy who treats his mother this badly is usually one who remains dependent, who is still a little boy inside, who has not developed any real self-confidence, any skills. And his mother has far more power than she imagines. Usually his anger and arrogance are covers for insecurity.

On the other hand, if she continues to accept his maltreatment of her, she will eventually lose his love. He needs to learn he cannot treat his mother that way and still have her provide a stocked refrigerator, keys to the car, clean clothes, a warm bed, the latest video games, a private chauffeur. And then he needs to develop some skills and competencies that will provide him with some self-esteem. This boy needs to spend a summer working with his uncle building houses.

"I think he has low self-esteem," the mother says of her 17 year-old son. She wants a therapist to help him with that. "Why should he have anything but low-self esteem?" I ask. "He is rude to you. He knows nothing. He has no skills. He has no jobs or chores or responsibilities. He steals and smokes dope. His self-esteem should be low. It is not counselling that will or should improve this. It is the insistence he behave better, and some form of real accomplishment, and **the necessity of assuming some responsibility.**"

Here is the question I might ask: The 16 year-old son of a single mother is asked to shovel the snow off the sidewalk. He is playing some video game. He grumbles, he makes excuses, he tells her "later". She asks again. The "later" becomes surly, defiant, rude. Mother gives up and takes the shovel in hand herself. Sitting in the armchair, controller in hand, the boy looks out the window and sees his mother cleaning the sidewalk. How does he feel? The answer is, he feels like shit. He feels upset with himself and his mother. His surliness will increase.

The same mother insists he shovel the walk. "Either you get your ass out there right now and clean that walk or the plug is pulled on your computer (I am not cooking your supper, not driving you to…)." The boy reluctantly puts on his sweater and takes shovel in hand. The sidewalk is now half clear. Breathing heavily in the winter sun, he leans on his shovel and looks at his work. How does he feel now? The answer is, not bad. Maybe even pleased with himself. His attitude will be improved when he comes in.

Of course I am not advocating a shouting match, or screaming at the kid. Just a simply stated consequence for not doing the job asked of him, and following through with the consequence without fanfare. The language you use to state that expectation is up to you. But the tone should be even, direct, clear, simple, devoid of anger if possible.

2.13 Boys and girls are different. Boys, when they turn about 15 or 16, become stupid. Girls, when they turn 13 or 14 become evil. Perhaps this is an exaggeration as well, to make a point, but the brains of boys and girls are different, the manner in which they approach the social world and problem-solve is different. Much of this is biological; some is social in origin.

When boys in a small group walk down to the shore of a lake you can be sure that within minutes one or all of the boys will throw something into the lake. That something may be a flat stone to skip across the lake, or the biggest object possible to make the biggest splash possible. That something may be one of the boys. This is effectance behaviour and you have been observing your boy-child engage in it since he was a toddler. (Of course if more than one boy throws a rock in the lake it will surely become a competition.)

If it can be opened he will open it; if it can be climbed he will climb it; if it can be pushed over he will push it over. He is programmed to create an effect. Pow, splash, bang. You hope that one day this impulse will be directed to building houses or fixing computers.

When girls in a small group walk down to that same lakeshore they will stand around and talk, usually about modes of conduct, dress, and relationships. They are organizing, adjusting, modifying, supporting their social world.

This is not to say that the boys don't talk and that girls will never throw a rock in the lake, but generally that is their pattern.

Girl brains tell their mouths to organize the social world; boy brains tell their muscles to do something. And sure, some boys can carry on a thoughtful conversation with an adult, though it won't usually be about the social organization of their peer group. And some girls will get together to do stuff rather than talk.

But when you have an adolescent in your household, or are about to have one, it is wise to anticipate and watch for the most common type of trouble to erupt.

So it should not be surprising that during a phase of development when aggressive, competitive, and sexual energies outstrip responsibility, empathy, logic, sequential reasoning, and the ability to hypothesize consequences, that girl talk can become manipulative, nasty, and cruel, and that boy behaviour can become stupid, ill-thought out, destructive, and dangerous. An extreme and tragic example occurred in Toronto recently: The 14 year-old girl thought another girl was a sexual competitor for the affections of her 17 year-old boyfriend. She asked him, cajoled him, blackmailed him into killing her rival. This he stupidly did.

Many parents say that, to their surprise, the boy was easier to raise than the girl. He tends to be in your face with his behaviour: rude, lewd, and crude, brash and noisy. It is easy to see what he's up to. And his schemes are quite simple. His lies are usually quite transparent. She, on the other hand, may be quite devious. She makes it harder to discern whose fault this is, who is doing what to whom. She can make utter nastiness appear to be a mood swing, someone else's fault, or a problem of low self-esteem. Her tears tug at your heart. His surly defiance irritates you. She's more verbal, quicker with the slick explanations and excuses.

These are all generalizations of course. Teachers report that more and more teenage girls are now resorting to physical violence. Of every teen who dies in a car accident two out of three are boys, but the girls are catching up. It's not just the boys who assault one another. The girls are now having physical showdowns in the parking lot. And some boys spend as much time as girls do gossiping on MSN and tending to their Facebook profile.

But, on the whole, it's what you can expect to have to deal with: subtle, scheming, manipulative behaviour from your daughter, and stupid, impulsive, sometimes aggressive behaviour from your son.

And if your child is gay, the reverse might be true.

2.14 Their behaviour tells the story. Most books on teens advise listening to them. Listen to what they have to say and learn ways of communicating with them. "Talk to your teenager," they all advise.

Okay. It's important at times, for an adolescent to feel that he is being heard, to know that someone is listening to him, that his ideas and opinions are respected, or at least **the fact that he has ideas and opinions** is respected. But this does not mean you have to believe him, or even entertain for a moment that his opinion is founded in experience, study, research, good judgement and self-awareness. So, yes, listen to them, but watch their behaviour. It is their behaviour that will tell you what they are really up to, what knowledge, skills and judgement they really possess. Talk to them, but **watch what they do, not what they say**.

They tell you about a problem. They emote about that problem, that other teen, the teacher, and the unfair expectations. You listen politely, and then, with great caution and sensitivity, you offer advice, of which you thought you were being asked. To your surprise you get a whiny, "You just don't understand." Followed by retreat to untidy bedroom and slammed door. Of course, you weren't being asked for advice at all. She just needed to let you know how unfair her life is. How teachers actually expect her to pay attention and do some work. How her peers can be just as egocentric as she is.

I remember the moment of peace and satisfaction that flowed from the time I got it right with my own daughter. It went something like this: We were driving along the highway, she in the passenger seat, not looking happy. Suddenly she launched into a litany of complaints about herself, her life, and her body. She had zits. She had no boyfriend. Her ankles were fat. Nobody liked her. Her face was a mess. She couldn't join the club she wanted. She hated school. She hated her brother. She might as well be dead.

When she paused to take a breath, I looked over and said, "Well, I love you Sweetie."

It was all that was required.

2.15 Raising teenagers has nothing whatever to do with trust. Well, it would be nice to trust them. It is what parents say: "I want to trust her." Or "I did trust her until…" or "It will be a while before she regains my trust."

As far as I can make out, 'trust' has to do with someone saying he or she will do, or not do something, in the future, and the listener being confident this will come to pass as stated. Or, the listener's (parent's) trust and confidence is that the adolescent will do (or not do) something that, in a sensible, civilized, caring, and thoughtful universe, would naturally come to pass or not come to pass from the unsupervised actions of said adolescent. It goes without saying.

But as pointed out earlier, the adolescent brain is in a state of flux. Loyalties have not been determined. Empathy for others is not developed. Consequences of action and inaction are unfathomable. The adolescent lives in the moment. And when she said, "I'll look after the house and the dog this weekend and I

58

won't have a party." You did not hear the unspoken **qualifiers** that went something like this: "Three or four of my friends is a group, not a party." And "If I just leave out enough food and water in the morning for the dog it won't matter when I get home." And, "If I invite a few friends over and then a hundred kids arrive, it isn't my fault."

So, no. It has nothing to do with trust. It has to do with observing their behaviour and from this knowing what to expect.

They will appeal to you, and look very hurt when you appear not to trust them. "Why don't you trust me now? – That happened when I was a kid." Or, my personal favourite, heard more than once, "Why don't you trust me? I haven't stolen nothing for a week."

When can you leave them in charge of the house for a weekend? When can you assume they are where they said they'd be on Saturday night? My guess? Somewhere around age twenty-five.

A mother called on the phone. She and her husband were planning a weekend away and her daughter, now 18, was pleading to be left in charge without a chaperone. "Do you think we can trust her?" asked the mother. In turn, I asked, "What happened the last time you left her alone?" The mother said, "We came home to five thousand dollars damage after a 200 person house party."

"There is your answer," I said.

My wife and I were planning a trip. The children no longer live at home. The oldest boy says, "Instead of Airways Transport to pick you up, I'll drive you to the airport."

"You'd have to pick us up by eight in the morning," I tell him. "The plane leaves at eleven."

"No problem," he says. "I'll be there." And I thank him for being so thoughtful and helpful.

Curiously, afterwards, his stepsister says, "I could have taken you. How come you never ask me?"

*They are both in their late twenties at this time. And, I realize, but do not say out loud, that this is probably the first time, and they have finally reached an age, when I can, if you'll pardon the word, **trust** that they will actually show up at the agreed upon hour and get us to the airport on time. It will be her turn next.*

He does arrive about twenty minutes late, but in my estimate of departure time, I have allowed for that.

I suggest forget 'trust'. It is usually foolish to 'trust' a teenager. Better to make a prediction of future behaviour based on observations of recent past behaviour. Continue to supervise until he or she **demonstrates** an ability to (drive the car safely, not drink and drive, look after the dog, look after the house without inviting in dozens of friends, go to a party without coming home stoned or drunk or high).

"But, mom, Alicia's parents will be there the whole time. I'll be fine." She tells you. You fear if you check this out, you will be showing a lack of 'trust'. Check it out anyway.

III. Owners' Maintenance Schedule

They didn't come with a manual, or even a link to a PDF file you could download. When he was a baby there were numerous grandmothers, aunts, friends, other new mothers, nurses, fathers, all ready to give advice, some of it very good. But not now. You suspect your neighbours are saying to one another, after witnessing or hearing a loud argument in your home, "If he was my kid I'd......". But they don't talk directly to you. They don't come to your door and give you advice. Your sister thinks you're too soft on the kid; your father thinks you should sign him up for Boy Scouts; your mother slips him extra money when he tells her how deprived he is. So for the most part, you are on your own with an adolescent.

And one size does not fit all. What works with one adolescent does not work with another. And each teen is living within, and is part of, a different circumstance, and a different family system.

When I was, say 12, 13, or 14, and displaying some surliness, my father would say, in his School Principal's voice, "Go outside and blow the stink off you." It worked for him and me. It may not work for you. At the same age, when my daughter arrived in the kitchen with the same surliness, I would tell her to go back to her bedroom until she could come down with a smile on her face. And ten minutes later she would re-emerge with, at least, a better attitude. But this might not work in your family.

So all I can give you are some general principals and ideas. Adapt them to your circumstances and cross your fingers. Here they are:

61

Your goal should be to get your adolescent child into adulthood, alive, healthy, preferably educated and skilled, without a major drug problem or criminal record or pregnancy. Anything more is icing and a pleasure to behold.

Without exception an adolescent **does not want** to always be in trouble, always be arguing with parents, always failing, always being yelled at, always being punished. They want to do better. They would rather succeed at school than fail. They would rather please you than not.

They do need to be yelled at sometimes, in trouble sometimes, disciplined sometimes. They need to fail at some things. They need to disappoint you occasionally, to feel guilt, to be a little ashamed of themselves at times. But not over and over again and always.

If that is happening then something is wrong. What is wrong may be your parenting or it may be something within the child that is preventing him from learning from your and his teacher's best efforts.

You are not the Waltons, Ozzie and Harriet Nelson, or Little House on the Prairies, or even the Huxtables. But for what it's worth, lets start with some ideals, and then move back to the real world.

The environment in which most adolescents would thrive would be this:

* Two parents who are happy with one another, each healthy, sane, enjoying their lives and work, in agreement with one another about child rearing, with time to spend having dinner together, playing with, watching over, and mentoring their kids.

* If the parents are not together, then two households sharing the kids, communicating easily, with set, organized times in each, and stability. Each of the two households functioning as described above.

* Good schools with good teachers and lots of resources.

* A neighbourhood without gangs and drug dealers.

* A community of resources.

* For the child who cannot be successful at the usual activities (school, sports, music), many alternative supervised activities and clubs and work.

* And a household that provides:

- Clearly stated expectations.

- Clearly and concretely stated house rules.

- Clearly stated and reasonable consequences for infractions of those rules.

- Consistent expectations and rules.

- Consistent application of the consequences for infractions.

- Time-limited and specific consequences.

- Clearly stated ways that the child might earn back a privilege he has lost.

- Each child given age-appropriate responsibilities.

- Everything beyond the basics of love, food, shelter, education, clothing, memberships, being earned in some way.

- Rewards and celebrations for that which should be rewarded and celebrated.

Maybe some families do live up to these ideals. On the other hand, living within this milieu might prove too stifling. I have a feeling that a teenager, living in this perfect environment, just might have to go out and get very drunk with his buddies and then push over a bus shelter.

So we must muddle through in the real world. It would definitely be easier to raise an ADHD kid in a Little House on the Prairies, or any teenage boy where the nearest saloon is a two-hour horseback ride away, or any teenage girl in a community that forbids electronics, insists on modesty of clothing, and milking the cows before breakfast.

But here is more practical advice:

1. Adolescent malfeasance can be divided, from a parent's point of view, into three categories:

i. That behaviour that deserves and requires no more than a rueful smile, a rolling of the eyes, a crinkling of the forehead, a sigh. This phase will pass. It's unimportant. He will learn eventually. This will be self-correcting.

ii. That behaviour that elicits nagging, counselling, explanations, irritation; that is, behaviour that requires you as a parent to do your duty and respond, to point out, to nag, to teach, **without any expectation that your nagging will make much difference now**.

"Pick up the bathroom towel." "Who was your maid before me?" "Will you not leave your sneakers in the middle of the floor." "Don't you have a project due on Friday?" "You'll ruin your supper." "Do you know how silly you look with orange hair?" "Will you turn that terrible music down please?"

There are two reasons to continue some (though not too much) of this teaching and nagging. The first reason is that most parents simply cannot stop doing it, at least not altogether. It is, after all, your duty to instruct your child in matters of manners, morals, cleanliness, tidiness, and good habits. Just don't overdo it and elicit a contrary or oppositional response, and then an unnecessary argument.

The second reason is that although your voice appears to be falling on deaf ears now, years from now you will have the pleasure of listening to your daughter repeat these same admonitions to her daughter. And, more seriously, while your advice and counsel may appear to have no impact now, you will probably find that your son and daughter, by the time they are thirty, have incorporated most of your values into their lives.

iii. And, finally, that behaviour that requires your swift action, perhaps with warnings but also with real consequences, ensuring compliance. In this case, what is needed are fewer words, clear statements, clear demands, backed up by real consequences that you are prepared to mete out.

There are some behaviours that should always fall into category **iii**. These include stealing, doing drugs, driving while drunk, disobeying a curfew, regular or prolonged truancy. And there are others that will depend on your personal and family values and tolerance.

But the point here is that as a parent you must decide. Is this a behaviour that must be stopped, prevented, dealt with by action? If so, it falls in category **iii**. and action is required, not argument, explanation, nagging: "You, my sweet, are grounded for one week. This means school, home, no Internet access, no cell phone, no unsupervised activities. And if you do that again, the next grounding will be two weeks."

Generally speaking if the teen is attending school, not skipping a lot, getting passing grades, not doing drugs or using alcohol, at least not in any persistent fashion, not stealing, almost always actually where you think he is or should be, engaged in some skill building supervised activity (from playing hockey to a part-time job), and home when he should be home, all the rest falls into categories one and two. As someone has said before, "Don't sweat the small stuff."

But do take action on the big stuff.

2. Don't try to be your teen's friend. She has friends. What she needs is a mother. You can become friends when she has grown up. Well, be her friend on those moments you can be, but always be ready to become her safe harbour and her MOTHER. As in **Motherrrrrr**.

We identify and often over-identify with the struggles of our teens. We often over-interpret their behaviour, seeking empathic and rational explanations. At one extreme the parent who remembers her own painful shyness and disappointments, her own sense of not being one of the popular crowd, may over-empathize with her daughter's angst and thus collude with school refusal and blaming the teachers. At the other extreme we have the father, who, remembering his teen years, and remembering saying no more than, "How high?" When his father said, "Jump." and who would never have dreamt of being disrespectful to his mother - he finds it totally unfathomable that his son ignores him and is rude to his mother.

The parents in both these extremes can be rendered ineffective. The mother who over-identifies will not see a sulk or a pout for what it really is, will be empathic to simple oppositional behaviour, will excuse obnoxious behaviour, and collude with avoidance and entitlement. The father who can't fathom how his son can be so different from himself as a teen, so rude, so careless, will find himself "sweating the small stuff", over-reacting to minor infractions, irritated by his son's dress and manner, constantly nagging, and then being totally ineffective when confronted by the big stuff.

3. Don't take it personally. Teens behave badly at times. They can be rude, disrespectful, and obnoxious. They have little empathy for you. Expecting them to have empathy for you, to be grateful for all you have done for them, for all the sacrifices you have made, is unrealistic. They may say they hate you, but they don't hate you. This is simply a very effective way of defeating you, at this moment, over this issue. The very intensity of the teen's opposition to you, the volume and degree to which he argues with you, are usually indicators of a strong bond. If he were **not** that attached to you, he would simply ignore you and drift away. Paradoxically, as mentioned before, the "seventeen year-old boys standing in the kitchen being rude to their mothers" are often momma's boys.

If you take their rudeness, their defiance personally, you will be easily defeated. Your guilt, and your fear of losing your son or daughter, will render you ineffective. And if you, out of guilt or low self esteem, or from simply being too tired and harried, allow your son to continue to be rude, obnoxious, defiant, and disrespectful, you will eventually lose him.

It appears to be such a common problem it bears repeating: Do not take your adolescent's behaviour and words, his misbehaviour and his verbal tirades, her nastiness and accusations, personally. If you can rise above it, knowing in your heart that you are a decent person and a good or at least adequate parent, you may be able to deal with the situation at hand effectively. If not, if she has seeded doubts about your self worth, if he has made you question your own power/authority, if she has made you feel guilty, if he has made you feel insecure, then you will not be effective dealing with the current situation.

To put it really clearly, when your son, having transgressed and been told he is grounded for one week, accuses you of being "the worst father in the world and a fucking bastard", the best response, with a calm smile on your face, is: "You're absolutely right, my son, but you are still grounded." An even more effective response is, if you do not have a problem with the language, "Naw. You're wrong. I'm worse than that. I'm a mother-fucking bastard, and you are still grounded." I did consider writing this as F dash, and M dash F dash, but the truth is, your teen is exposed to this language, and probably uses this language readily, and if he can upset you by using it, you have lost your edge; you will be rendered ineffective. To be able to deal with this boy effectively his language must not find its target. You must let it roll off your back.

When you hear that phrase, "How dare you talk to your father like that?" issue from your lips, you are in trouble.

But, you say, I will be modelling the use of bad language. Well, yes and no. Remember his need to imitate and oppose. Maybe he will imitate you. Maybe he will oppose. I used the F word quite loosely. My son, in my presence, took to substituting the word 'Frig'. When he was 17 I asked him, on a warm summer day, to come share a beer with me. He said, "I don't drink, dad. I'll have a pop." Now it was a small lie. Or one of those statements with tacit qualifier, the qualifier being, "with my parents." But it does speak to that complex need to oppose, to separate, rather than blindly imitate.

All right, if you can't tolerate that kind of language in your household perhaps you could find a way of eliminating it pre-teens: systems of rewards for good language, and minor punishments for your child when he uses the F word. But in those teenage years, deducting twenty-five cents from the weekly allowance for each profanity will probably not work. And the last thing you want to do with a teenager is decree a law of the land that you cannot enforce. **You don't want to ever engage in an argument with a teen that you can't win.**

And keep in mind, with such decrees, that teenagers are always on high alert for hypocrisy, and always willing to point it out to you.

Deep in their hearts they do not want to win these battles; they do not want to be so ugly and rude and get away with it. For if they

68

consistently win, if they consistently wander in late with no consequences, refuse to help with no consequences, they will feel badly about themselves, they will not like themselves, they will feel they are losing their parent's love and respect, they will feel they do not have a parent strong enough to control their outrageous impulses, and thus, **they will not feel safe**.

So set the rule; apply the consequence for infraction; ignore the display of displeasure they must offer up before giving in; feel good about it; you have made your son or daughter feel safe and secure. And it will show later.

4. You have perspective. Your teen may believe, and tell you, that certain things and events are essential for her health, welfare, her very existence on this planet, such as the right lipstick, getting a call from a certain boy, not wearing a coat, going to the concert this Friday night, wearing a certain blouse, having a cell phone, having a cell phone with a pale blue cover, going on MSN tonight. You know these are **not** essential for her health and welfare. YOU ARE RIGHT. And though, when these things are denied, she will emote, it will be forgotten within a few hours. You have perspective, experience, and knowledge. She does not.

5. On the other hand, don't lose perspective. If your teenager is attending school, not using drugs, not over-indulging in alcohol, not on probation or parole, not stealing, has a couple of friends, is either not sexually active or at least using protection – if he or she is doing all of the above but showing lack of motivation or direction (which is most annoying to accomplished parents) this may simply be a phase.

He or she may shut down when you try to give him direction. He may spend far too much time playing video games. She may spend far too much time gossiping with friends. You might be able to nudge your teen into spending less time hanging out and more time engaged in productive activities, but if he or she is attending and passing school, and not really doing anything bad, immoral, or illegal, it might be time to abide, while remaining alert. Motivation and interest can only take root when the brain is ready, and confidence high.

We can lose perspective. I think it must relate to the last point. We are taking the child's attitude, his lack of respect, his lack of ambition, personally. Or we might actually be projecting our own failures and worries into the teen. The father who overreacts badly when his son plays an inept and lazy hockey game for example. It is not really the son who has caused this parental outburst. No. It is the father's memories of his own adolescent sloth and missed opportunities.

My first lesson regarding losing perspective came many years ago. The 16 year-old boy was on probation for stealing. He had been doing drugs. He was truant from school. Six months later he was back at school, not doing drugs, off probation, coming home when he was supposed to. But the parents, especially the father, were still angry with him. I asked why. He's at school. He's passing, doing his homework. Off probation. Not stealing. Not doing drugs as far as we can tell. Why are you still so angry with him?

"Well," said the father. "Just look at his hair." This would be about 1973. The boy's hair was long, as indeed was my own. "He needs a haircut," said the father. "He'll never get a job with hair like that. But he refuses to get it cut."

6. There really is no need for prolonged arguments. The issue will lie within one of the three categories above. For the first category you should roll your eyes and opt out. For the second you should remind or nag once or twice or thrice and then roll your eyes and opt out. For the third, your action is required, not your words.

Many parents come into the counselling session saying, "My child and I are always arguing." They want the counsellor to help the child stop arguing, failing to notice that an argument requires the active participation of at least two people. You are the adult; she is a child. Perhaps a little discussion is appropriate; perhaps allowing the child to express his or her point of view is appropriate; but either the thing that you want him or her to do, or not do, is important or unimportant. If unimportant, take a pass. If important, why should there ever be an argument? The parental request or order is stated. The child complies or doesn't comply. An age appropriate consequence for failure to comply follows.

I do admit the above paragraph is somewhat idealistic. Life is more complicated. As parents we can all be drawn into arguments with our teens. It might not be so simple to decide if the issue is important or unimportant. We might be tired and irritated and stressed. The adolescent might be quite tenacious. In fact, the adolescent's purpose or motivation may be the argument itself – that is, the ostensible object of the argument might be a red herring. The teen's goal may be to simply engage you. He is defining himself, his ideas, and his values. He needs your reaction in order to be oppositional.

On the first warm spring day of the year, the boy comes into the back yard where his mother and stepfather are barbecuing. The boy says, "There's this new way of growing marijuana. You put it in sacks and hang it from trees and it can't be detected from the air. Is it okay if I try some this summer?"

The stepfather says, "Chris, what do you think my answer has to be?"

Chris says, "You have to say 'no', I guess."

"Okay." Says the stepfather, "If you know I have to say no, why are you asking?"

"Well," says Chris, "There's this new way of growing marijuana and I want to try it."

"But think about it." Says the stepfather. "If you already know I must say "NO", why do you think you're still standing there asking the question?"

"Because there's this new way of growing Marijuana and........."

The stepfather is on his game that night. But he's asking Chris a question Chris cannot yet understand. He's asking him to think about the process of the communication, the meta-message, the boy's own real motivation for asking the question. The stepfather also knows that a simple, "Certainly not." could illicit questions of "Why not?" followed by arguments about the decriminalisation of marijuana and the comparative health risks and benefits of marijuana vs. the glass of Scotch in stepfather's right hand. The argument could get quite testy, encroach on other issues, and end with stepson storming off to seek commiseration and validation from his buddies. The stepfather was trying to get the boy to see how he was simply angling for this predictable argument, even though the script is already written. But the boy cannot do this yet. His ability to observe and analyse his own thinking and behaviour is limited.

7. Know when you have won. You have learned your son skipped school today. Still, he expects to borrow the car and go to a party tonight. You have told him he may not have the car and he may not go out because he skipped school. In his anger at this he has called you something (Hitler, dinosaur, psycho-bastard, lousy father) – and what he called you, may hurt. But here is your best answer: "That may be true, but you are still not getting the car and you are still grounded."

Reviewing these encounters with unhappy parents we frequently find the following has occurred: The teen has transgressed in some way. The parent, perhaps not in the best unemotional, neutral fashion, has applied a consequence. The child argues. The parent stands firm (perhaps again with too many decibels, but firm nonetheless). "No. You may not go out tonight. Period." The child has a tantrum, yells and screams a little, calls the parent a name, storms off, slams the door to his or her bedroom. Perhaps the child has shouted a particularly pointed barb on her way to her bedroom. They are good at this.

Now, at this point, you've actually done your job as a parent. The child has transgressed. You have applied a consequence. The child has gone to her room. It is time to return to watching CSI or whatever you were doing. You've won. The point has been made, the lesson learned. That she did not accept the consequence gracefully is not important at this time. That is a lesson to be learned later in life.

But many parents cannot resist following this teen to her room to either a.) Admonish her further for her foul attitude, b.) Try to get her to accept her punishment with a smile so the parent won't feel guilty. Or c.) Reason with the child, convince her you are just doing your duty and school is important and there will be another day to hang out with her friends.

Now, when the parents do this they are showing their cards; they are showing the teen they are not sure of themselves; their resolve is weak. They are also reopening an argument they have already won. This is going to go downhill fast. Admonishing her further for her foul attitude may lead to outright defiance and storming out of the house. Trying to reason with the child may open a whole mess of problems ("You just don't understand.") and ruin your entire evening.

Leave it. You have asserted your authority, done your duty. Tomorrow is another day and another challenge.

As the years go by, if you are lucky, you and your ex-teen will have little talks, opportunities to reminisce. She may say, "Remember that time you were sure you had three quarters of a bottle of Scotch left and you couldn't figure out how it got down to one quarter?" or "Remember that time I was dating the sheet metal worker and….?" Or "Remember that time I came home stoned and I swore up and down that I had never used anything stronger than marijuana?"

> *Long into her adulthood my daughter reminisced about the time she stuck her head into my attic studio and told me, with all the vitriol a child can muster, that I was a lousy, lousy father and that she hated me. "Thank goodness," she said. "You didn't take me seriously and you didn't react at all." It may have been dumb luck or preoccupation that kept me from reacting, that kept me from pursuing her to confront her disrespect, or to try to find out why "she hated me", but leaving it alone was clearly the right path at the time. She had to vent her unhappiness about some action I had taken or not taken. That was it. There was no need to reopen the issue, whatever that issue had been.*

8. It is your household. You pay the mortgage. You buy the food, pay the phone bill. You decide which behaviours fall into which of the categories listed at the top of this section.

At the turn of the last century children were "seen but not heard." The parents were definitely head of the household. Very little bad behaviour would be tolerated. In affluent households, boys might be sent to boarding schools for the better part of their childhood and adolescence. Girls would be schooled in feminine arts and early on betrothed. In poorer households, boys would be apprenticed or sent out to work by their teens or even earlier, and girls married off. A writer and scholar of the era wrote in his memoirs that his wife and he had had "twelve or thirteen" children. It seems astounding that he wasn't sure of the number, but then, at that time, children often died in birth or a few years later. Parents could not afford to place in each and every one the emotional investment we offer our one, two, and, occasionally, three children today.

The pendulum has swung a long way in the western world, and especially in North America. Today's households often appear entirely child-centred, the schedules of the family organized around the child's activities and wishes. Some parents find the right balance, or at least a balance that works for them, giving their children every possible opportunity to develop skills and ambitions and independence while keeping ego-centricity, omnipotence, and entitlement, in check. Offering them voice and opinion but not a power for which they are not ready.

Every 12 months or so an article appears in the newspaper about parents who have gone on strike. They camp in the front yard or back yard and erect signs that read, "On Strike", "No More Cleaning, Cooking or Driving." If it goes on long enough, a reporter interviews them. They say they'll go back to work if their kids start doing some of the chores they are asked to do, like cleaning their rooms. The reporter then interviews Child Agency spokespersons, and the teenagers in question. The parents say nothing else has worked, maybe a little humiliation and embarrassment will. The Agencies fret that the children will be placed at risk. The children are embarrassed for their parents.

Curiously, staying with the management/workers metaphor, these parents do not see themselves as Management. They are workers demanding better conditions, a few concessions. Unfortunately, the newspapers don't carry short or long-term outcome reports on these family crises. So we don't know if going on strike worked, or if simply a few concessions were made and the parents returned to their roles as indentured servants. Or if Children's Services swept in and restored the children to their rightful thrones.

Teenagers taking over and running the household would appear to be a uniquely North American problem, perhaps beginning to spread to Europe. In our headlong rush to ensure our children have all possible opportunities to grow and succeed, to develop a strong sense of esteem and worth, we sometimes give them too much authority and power. They may insist on it. They may demand it. But they are not ready for it. Their anxiety increases as their safety net decreases and then they act badly.

The mother and fourteen year-old girl have been waiting half an hour for their appointment with the child psychiatrist. He is late, having spent some extra time with another family. The mother approaches the desk. With a worried look on her face she tells the receptionist that her daughter is becoming very upset that she has to wait so long.

The parents of a teen tell me that their routine on both Friday and Saturday night is to wait for a phone call from their daughter to tell them where she is so they can go pick her up. She is supposed to phone by midnight. "Every Friday and Saturday?" I ask. The answer is, "Yes".

"So though you've both worked all day Friday, and you are tired, and you've had a couple of glasses of wine with dinner, and you want to go to bed, or watch a movie, you get in the car at midnight to fetch your daughter every week?" I ask.

"We don't mind doing that," they tell me. "What we mind is she doesn't call till twelve-thirty or one and then she's not where she said she'd be. By the time we get there she's moved on to some other place and we have to go looking for her."

Clearly the power structure in these two families is off kilter. Perhaps in the first example the mother has been rendered impotent and helpless by the daughter's threat of emotional outbursts in public, or she is afraid of the classic teen line: "I hate you." I understand that the teenager feels she is the centre of the universe, that her time is more valuable than that of a doctor, that time moves slowly for her, and she has no patience. The problem is the mother has accepted this version of reality, and thus has enabled her daughter's entitlement, her omnipotence. And this is probably THE PROBLEM in the family.

In the second example, the child's safety will be mentioned as the reason these parents have become chauffeurs-on-demand, on call long past union hours. But this child is learning all the wrong lessons: Her time, her instant gratification, her pleasures are far more important than any discomfort her parents might feel. The omnipotence she displayed as a two year-old is being rekindled by her mom and dad's servitude. She will begin to lose friends. She will begin to feel unsafe, unprotected. She may truly begin to dislike her victimized mother and father. For it is well known that we humans dislike the people we find we can walk over, or humiliate. We don't respect people who show no respect for themselves. These parents, with the best of intentions, will bring about, by their actions, the very circumstance they are afraid of: the child will dislike them, not respect them, pay no attention to their warnings and admonitions, engage in risky behaviour, and feel unsafe.

So keep them safe, support all their initiatives to grow and develop, support them just having fun now and again, but do not sacrifice your own comfort, values, pleasures, at least not unless they have earned this privilege. They don't need servants. They do not need to party, socialize, or hang out as much as they feel they do. They need parents they can respect and admire. It may even come to pass that their plans have to change to accommodate their mother's and father's social life. Heaven forbid.

As Dr. Cliff Huxtable once said to his son Theo, in one of the few modern sitcoms that occasionally portrayed parents as sane and sensible adults, "When you start paying the mortgage on this house, then you can decide ……."

IV. Troubleshooting

All right. You are doing your best and your teenager is still out-of-control, or in retreat, or defiant, oppositional, doing drugs, skipping school, depressed, miserable, stealing, ignoring curfew etc. **Is it your parenting or is something wrong with your child?**

Owner/operator error

Your teen is behaving badly. You are paying attention to his bad behaviour. But you have limited time and a lot of other things on your mind, so when you look back, you see that the only time you pay any attention, the only time when you communicate with him at all, is when he is behaving badly. Even the manuals for training puppies tell us this is wrong. You need to spend at least as much time, if not more, waiting for good behaviour, noticing it, rewarding it. Pre-teenage years this might have required nothing but a smile, and a "Good job, Jonny." In his teens it could take more than that: the proverbial going fishing together, and setting jobs, and chores, and goals with financial rewards.

You think you are consistent, but you are not. You warn and warn but seldom follow through. And when you do it is out of anger and over-the-top. Or the parents argue about what would be an appropriate expectation or punishment, leaving a gap or a non-decision through which most teenagers could drive a truck, or an all night party.

You think you are strict, and, in fact the child is complaining that you are too strict, but the truth is you don't follow through. You just yell and complain and nag a lot. Being overly strict is seldom a problem. As I'm fond of pointing out, you can raise a perfectly good citizen on a Mennonite Farm. The problem more commonly is **failed strictness, failed authority**.

For many possible reasons, nobody is actually saying STOP, or unplugging the computer, or monitoring the time spent on the cell phone, or taking away the cell phone (video game, television), watching curfew, paying attention to what the child is up to, insisting on a few chores being completed, monitoring attendance at school.

The seventeen year-old girl saw the counsellor alone before we saw the parents. She told the counsellor the problem was her parents were too strict, way too strict, too controlling. After all, she's seventeen. She said her Saturday night curfew was nine o'clock. All her friends could stay out later. Wasn't nine unreasonable at seventeen?

The counsellor nodded empathically. Nine o'clock, seventeen, a little early. She reported to the team that this was a child with over-controlling parents.

But here is what really happened, discovered when the child and her parents were interviewed in the room together: The girl's curfew on Saturday night had been midnight. But she was drifting in later and later during the few weeks before this appointment, eventually coming in at 1:30 A.M. The father confronted her and reiterated the midnight curfew. The following Saturday the girl arrived home at 2 A.M. Sunday morning. The parents were waiting up. The father lost his temper in the ensuing argument. "From now on," he told his daughter, "You'll be home by nine on Saturday."

You may be allowing your teen (having been told to respect her opinion and decisions) far too much freedom and choice. She craves it; she wants it; she demands it; but she is not ready for it.

The out-of-control teen may be emotionally over her head and reacting to this. She is conspiring with her friends 24/7 on MSN. She is sexually active, meaning she is engaged in a powerful, intimate, yet confusing and frightening activity with a passing lout who may or may not have eyes for six of her other friends, or he may be a boy with the poetic intensity of Romeo. She might be trying to rescue a friend who is threatening suicide.

When this teen cuts herself, or emotes vigorously, angers easily, cries throbbingly, she is asking her parents to rescue her. This they should do by assuming control of portions of her life. She will begin to settle down and smile (after protestations), and she may even thank her parents when she turns 32. This is a fairly common scenario. The child is said to have mood swings, up one minute, down the next, giggling and then angry, happy she has a new boyfriend, then sitting at the computer at one AM and cutting her arms, while texting about this event to her four closest friends and the ex-boyfriend.

Her mood control system is immature, highly reactive, and she is over her head, overwhelmed. Her moods are indeed swinging rapidly, but not because of a bipolar disorder, but because she can't handle all that she has taken on. She does not yet have the internal resources, the brain development and experience, which will enable her to safely manage all that she has taken on. In lieu of adequate internal monitors, control, perspective, she needs external control and boundaries.

The boy on some self-destructive course of alcohol, surliness, and risky behaviour, is also waiting for someone to say STOP. Often this boy is waiting for Dad to say stop, as in "**STOP**!"

This may pose a dilemma for a single female parent trying to raise a 16 year-old boy. There is no getting around it, when it comes to boys, fathers have something my son used to call, "Dad Power". He was 18 and athletic. Still, I could usually take him one on one at a basketball net, using guile and a little roughness. He should have been beating me every time. "Dad Power" he called it, referring I think, to the natural reluctance a boy will have to play rough, to bump and cheat and go all out against the Father. He doesn't really want to beat his dad, not yet. I think Freud would smile at this.

So when it comes to curbing his son's behaviour, a father has an edge, should he choose to use it. Without doubt they respond better to a firm male voice than to a tentative or angry soprano. On the other hand, boys may also respond better to a firm, certain female voice than to an uncertain or overly angry male voice.

Much has been written about the absence of the father in the contemporary teenage boy's life. "All over America there are 17 year-old boys standing in the kitchen being surly to their mothers." The father, gone from the home, or simply working late at the office, is not there. He is not there as a role model, sharing and teaching skills. He is also not there to say STOP.

Many of the boys we see in trouble either have no father, see their father occasionally at their own discretion or whim, or have exceedingly passive fathers, or fathers who have been pushed out of the parenting role. Or a stepfather who could act, but has decided, or been told, to stay out of the parenting role.

Sometimes getting the boy's behaviour under control has been simply a matter of treating the father's depression, or giving the stepfather a green light to intervene. Unfortunately, at other times, there is a father at home, but he is too busy struggling with his own addictions, alcoholism, unemployment, unhappy marriage, or depression, to pay enough attention to his son.

Jason, a fourteen-year-old adopted son of two professionals, was in trouble. He was constantly surly with his parents, skipping school, and ignoring curfew. He was suspected of using marijuana on occasion, and perhaps stealing. Some ADHD contributed to his problems with judgment and impulse control. But both parents wanted to understand him. They desperately wanted to see him happy.

82

The father withdrew from any sternness, any forceful assertions.

Neither parent appeared capable of believing their son might not be telling the truth. So when the father asked, "Jason, what's that new bicycle doing in our back yard?" and Jason answered, "Oh, that's Neville's. He didn't wanna ride it home and asked me to keep it overnight for him." the father believed this. He did allow a small doubt to creep into his mind when the second new bicycle appeared in the back yard. And when Jason was stopped in a car with older boys and all were charged with possession of marijuana and Jason explained that it wasn't his, and he never smoked the stuff, and the smell of marijuana on his clothing was from the other kids toking up, his father believed him.

But the police did catch Jason with stolen property, and he was charged with theft. A creative judge sentenced him to community service, specifically, that under the supervision of his father and a police officer, Jason would paint an entire room at the local police station. This entailed the father waking his son early in the morning, taking him to the hardware store to buy paint and rollers, and then taking him to the police station. Jason painted the room to the police officer's satisfaction and his father's amusement.

A week after this event I saw the parents. The mother expressed astonishment that for the past week Jason had been "chipper", looking happier than she had seen him in months. She couldn't understand this.

Well, it seemed clear enough to me. Someone had finally said STOP. His father had, albeit reluctantly, asserted some authority (with help), and Jason had actually done something useful, something he could look at proudly.

*Hence, his anxiety was lower, he felt safer, and he didn't
need to display attitude, at least not for a week or so.*

*One mother wanted, most of all, that her 15 year-old son
stop abusing her verbally, stop telling her to "Fuck off." We
reviewed the last time he did this, when she had asked him to
do some small thing, and he had responded with a surly,
"Fuck off." And then I asked what she had done next. "Well,
it was Wednesday night so I drove him to his hockey
practice," she said. When I asked, with some incredulity,
why on earth she had chauffeured him to hockey after his
nasty remark, the mother broke down in tears and said, "I
can't deprive him of hockey. He loves it so much."*

*Another mother told me her son had stolen her bank
card and taken $1500 from her account. He had been caught
on surveillance camera and been charged. The mother then
gave a lawyer a $5000 retainer to defend her son in court.*

*"So let me get this straight," I said. "Someone steals
fifteen hundred dollars from you and then you spend five
thousand dollars defending him? Have I got that right?"*

*"When you put it that way, it does sound a little crazy",
said the mother.*

In each of these three cases it is also worth asking, "Exactly
what is it we are trying to teach these children?"

Not infrequently single mothers enter the office with their
fourteen-year-old girls, looking like they belong to different
cultures or income groups. The girl is all decked out in designer
clothing, adorned with jewellery, face painted, hair multi-coloured,
IPOD and cell phone at hand; the mother is all Value Village: old
track pants, cheap blouse, no makeup, running shoes, hair that has

84

not seen a salon in ten years. The mother is worried about her daughter staying out all night, dropping out of school, and dating nineteen-year-old boys. She is worried her daughter has low self-esteem.

It is often difficult in mother/daughter relationships to figure out where one begins and the other ends, who is feeling what, what is fact, what is interpretation, what is projection. Who is it in this room who really has the low self-esteem? These mothers are often trying to be a friend to their daughters, making sure they don't miss out on whatever the mother feels she has missed out on, enjoying life and having fun in a manner the mother feels she no longer can. But these girls get ahead of themselves, emotionally and behaviourally out-of-control. They need a parent who can say NO, who can limit them, whose own self-esteem allows this.

Here is a short list of the ways we parents fail, from the simplest to correct to the most difficult:

1. You understand your teen. You know what you should be doing. You simply need support and encouragement to do the right thing.

Teen culture itself weighs against you. North American culture weighs against you. Most television sit-coms, which in a sense are today's morality plays, depict fathers as loveable buffoons, and mothers as mediators, and children as the clever ones. Your son points out how his friends are allowed to .... Your daughter appears mature, at times. They tell you they cannot live without a cell phone, a certain article of clothing, constant access to MSN. "Everybody's doing it." "It's not as though I'm using chemicals." "Jason's mom is really cool." "You're so old fashioned."

Consider this book support and encouragement to do the right thing. Other help can be found with friends, counsellors (for you, not your teen), family doctor, and parenting groups.

You know that when your son used your car and came home drunk, he should be denied access to that car for at least a few months, and that when you once again allow him access you should make sure no drinking will be involved. Do it.

You know your daughter should not be allowed to party Friday night after skipping most of her classes during the week. Say no. And once you have said "No." the only thing you might say next is, "What part of 'No' did you not understand?"

You know, well, you know that your adolescent's **privileges should be earned,** their **malfeasance should be, in some way, punished,** and that **responsibility will not be learned unless it is expected.** Your teen will relax when he knows the rules and understands they are **definite, consistent, and non-negotiable.**

2. You don't have a way of understanding your teen. You are confused by his behaviour. You are getting conflicting advice. "It's just a phase." "Teens are different today." "They know so much more than we did." You have been using reason and compromise to no avail. If you understood where his behaviour was coming from, you could deal with it. You assume, because he is both smart and basically good, that he will make smart choices and avoid doing anything immoral or illegal. Because he is both smart and good you assume he will listen to your explanations of long-term consequences. You don't have a way of understanding the limitations of his adolescent brain. You may be applying an adult template in your attempts to understand his behaviour.

The remedy for this is to re-read chapter one of this book.

3. Your teen comes from another planet. She is not at all like you were as a teen. You would never have talked back to your father. You would never have disrespected your mother. You did your chores, went to school, joined Girl Guides, didn't date until you were 17, helped with the dishes and raising your younger brother. All **your** mother had to do was raise her eyebrows and you fell in line.

So your child was born with a different temperament. She is more outgoing, risk-taking. She tests boundaries, challenges authority. This is not necessarily bad, simply different. Ultimately, as an adult, she may enjoy a more interesting life than you, providing she doesn't have a teenage pregnancy or acquire an addiction. She is also growing up in a different era, with different expectations, with more information **of a kind** at her disposal, usually with far more discretionary income.

The place to start with this teen is to accept that she is not you. You have different temperaments. And temperaments are those mostly inherited personality traits that fall somewhere within the continuums of:

Extraverted .... Introverted

Risk Taking .... Cautious and Avoidant

High Energy........................... Low Energy

Very Curious........................ Neo-phobic

Add to this the understanding of the adolescent brain from Chapter One and you have your teen. But it is not easy seeing your teen do things you would never have done. You felt horribly guilty the one time you lied to your mother. Your daughter seems to be without remorse. All the talk, ideas, arguments, values, thoughts and feelings that governed your behaviour as a child fall on deaf ears with your own teenager. She is not you. You will have to approach her with a new set of skills.

4. Your child is all too much like you as a boy. And you did okay eventually. He'll get through this. He's just sowing his wild oats.

This may be true both as fact and prophecy. But, the times have changed. The consequences of not having an education may be more severe. The drugs available are more addictive and more debilitating. The sexually transmitted diseases are less treatable. The skills required to earn a good living are more complex. Maybe his brain will click in at age 26 or so, like yours did, but a little vigilance, a little guidance and correction, may be required to get him to that age without severe addictions or criminal record and enough competencies to earn a living.

I was seeing the Native Canadian father of several children after his oldest son got drunk and high on gas sniffing, and shot off his rifle at a few other teens one night on the reserve. The boy was now in jail. The father was an imposing, powerful man. I had talked with him about how we might try to keep his son out of trouble when he was released from jail. "It is not the Indian way," he said, "to discipline our children. They must learn on their own, find their own way. I was the same at his age."

I was aware that there had been no road to his reserve when the father was growing up. It had been far more isolated. I told him I was sure that way of raising children must have been fine years ago, in an isolated village. But today the kids have access to alcohol, drugs, gasoline, firearms, and junk food. They have far more ways of getting into trouble. (I thought I might be going over the top mentioning junk food, but I could have included RAP lyrics, TV, the Internet, and violent video games). The father told me it was a common problem on the reserve and arranged

for me to meet with the Band Council. When I met with the
Band Council we talked of many things, the rampant
alcoholism on the reserve, the complexity of governing a
small nation within a nation, and they all agreed that their
teenagers were out-of-control, terrorizing the reserve on
Saturday night, much too often ending up in jail, or brain
damaged from gas sniffing, or dead. "It is the parents'
fault," one Councillor said. "They do not discipline their
children."

In the city, on a reserve, in the suburbs, our teenagers live in a different world than we did. It may "take a village to raise a child" but it takes a parent to keep them away from guns, and gas, and booze, and drugs, and to see that they are home at night and in school during the day.

5. You and your spouse don't agree on how to deal with your son's behaviour.

Your background is very different than dad's. Trying to deal with your son always leads to arguments between you, of which, your son, as any good teenager will do, takes advantage.

The boy is just thirteen. The parents cannot agree on
anything about him. They cannot agree on school
expectations, curfew, chores, cleaning his room. I search for
some area they can agree on. He drinks too much coffee,
says mother. Father agrees with this. So I seize coffee
drinking as a starting point. How can these two parents limit
the boy's coffee drinking? Mostly he drinks coffee at home,
from the pot mother makes for herself and her husband, or
sometimes for her son. We discuss this. I ask them then to
turn to the boy together and tell him clearly and specifically
that "Henceforth, he shall not help himself to the coffee
mother makes for his parents, and she will no longer brew a

second pot for him. He will not drink coffee at home." The mother does this. The boy listens. The father is hesitating. I ask him to reiterate to his son the directive just now delivered by the boy's mother. The father instead says, "You know, I'm not so sure there's anything wrong with a kid drinking coffee."

Somehow, for these two parents, their own conflict, or their own power struggle, precludes them ever agreeing on any directive or rule or consequence for their child. Most children and teens are programmed to take advantage of conflicted parenting. They know which parent to ask about which issue. If the parents cannot agree on a curfew being nine or ten or anything at all, then the child will know he can stay out as late as he pleases. This parental conflict will have to be addressed, at least partially, if these parents are going to learn to be even a little bit effective as parents.

It is a common problem. The parents disagree. One is strict, the other is not. One is the disciplinarian; the other is the buddy, the friend. It can still work if the easy-going parent backs up the disciplinarian and if any disagreements about how to handle a situation are discussed and resolved privately.

Sometimes it is just a matter of knowing this: that it is more important for the parents to be on the same page than finding the perfect or exactly right way of responding. And generally, of course, if there is a good default position, it is the stricter of the two.

But when parents disagree on parenting the problem can be more complex and less amenable to advice. The disagreement may be but a symbolic expression of a deeper power struggle. As in the "coffee" example above, these parents cannot agree on anything.

Then it is time for the counsellor to say, "Next session, why not leave Kyle at home and just the two of you come in?"

6. Some health or life problems are distracting you, throwing you off your game.

The mother is ill. The father is depressed. The father just got laid off. Money is running out. A grandmother is dying. It can be very distressing for parents, at times like these, to discover their teenager, instead of showing empathy and pitching in to help, is demanding more and taking advantage of his parents' distractions.

Do not expect adult empathy, or a mature and responsible attitude at these times. If it happens it is very nice. But do not expect it.

In these situations we need to help the parents, to what extent possible, to regain their health, their composure, their strength and resources, so they can apply appropriate parenting. Occasionally, when the teenage boy is out-or-control the solution is to treat the father's depression.

7. Your relationship is in transition, in upheaval. A separation is coming. Divorce. You are already living apart but still fighting.

While the parents struggle to define their own relationship, the teen, even while sad and angry about losing one or both parents, and losing his fantasy of a normal, happy home, may be given far too much freedom and responsibility. He may be allowed to drift between the parents, having always to choose one and disappoint the other. Apart or together, parents still need to be parents. Here are three rules-of-thumb for separated parents:

i. You, the parents, decide how to share the kid(s). You make the schedule. You make the arrangements. Do not allow your teenager to drift between the parents, or run from one to the other to avoid a certain set of rules.

"The door is always open for him to come see me." is not good enough. The part-time parent needs to insist the child be with him on specific nights or weekends. A loose arrangement, or letting the kids decide, leaves them with impossible choices, such as: 'if I go with Dad this weekend, Mother will look hurt', 'shall I disappoint Dad, or miss hanging out with my three best friends and keep up with the latest gossip?' Given these kinds of choices, the child's anxiety will rise, and you will see attitude, sadness, and bad behaviour.

ii. If the teenager is now being shared by two households, what goes on in one is not the business of the other. One may be stricter than the other. Teenagers can handle this. The thirteen year-old girl knows she needn't tell her mother what a great time she had on the weekend with Dad's new girlfriend. Don't ask about it. You will never be replaced. Focus on your relationship with your kids. If the two households get to the point of being able to communicate with one another in a healthy and civilized manner, all the better.

iii. Allow the new stepparent to be a parent. Perhaps that cannot be achieved after a certain age, but usually (not always of course) the stepparent sees the teenager's behaviour quite clearly and knows what should be done. The biological parent's judgment is often clouded by love, fear, and guilt.

8. You simply do not have the financial and/or emotional resources to deal with a badly behaved teen. Your fifteen year-old son is smoking marijuana daily, skipping school, hanging out with a bad crowd, and experimenting, you suspect, with other drugs. Wouldn't it be nice if you had the resources and freedom to throw him into the back seat of the car, hitch up the trailer, and take him on a two month canoeing and camping trip? But it is unlikely you can do that.

A single working mother and a sixteen-year-old boy who comes and goes as he pleases, who drops out of school and smokes marijuana all day is a more common situation.

She can't discipline him; she can't demand of him; she can't assert her own rights because she is afraid of losing his love. She might even be afraid of him in other ways. Or she has to work the evening shift at the factory and literally cannot supervise her son's comings and goings, the gatherings he has in her house.

This parent needs help from relatives, friends, community resources, counsellors and therapists. Ultimately she may need help from the police, the courts, and the boy's probation officer.

9. You, unfortunately, need the distraction of your adolescent's bad behaviour. The parents argue about their child's behaviour all the time. They constantly argue with the child, without effect or resolution. It is a distraction from their own conflict, their own failed relationship. Indeed, they need their child to behave badly to prevent them having to face the barrenness or conflict in their own relationship. Family therapists talk of such a badly behaved child as being the glue that holds the family together. This is another moment when the therapist might say, "Let's leave Kyle at home next appointment and just the two of you come in."

10. Your child's problem is really your problem. Sometimes the parent's mental illness or addiction is the real problem. The child is merely reacting to this, perhaps doing the best he or she can. The roles within the family may be reversed, with the boy trying his best to look after his alcoholic mother, or protect his depressed father. In family systems the member who is identified as having the problem is sometimes merely the **symptom carrier**. The actual problem may reside in someone else.

11. You are inventing the problem. Occasionally the child is simply a projection of the parent's wishes and fears. That is, the parent's own fears, anxieties, delusions and distortions, are projected into, or displaced onto, the child. The parent tells us how bad the child is, how wilfully malevolent, how evil, while the teacher is saying what a nice, helpful student he is. But he is a teen; he is attached to this parent; he may find himself fulfilling his parent's expectations, at least at home. "You're just like your father. You're no good. You're going to end up in jail and go straight to hell."

This parent needs psychiatric help.

V. Workarounds

It is wise to remember that your job is to get your adolescent alive and well into adulthood, not addicted, without criminal record, not pregnant, and preferably educated. All the rest that you wish for would be nice but is not necessary. There obviously are some children who can be moulded into hockey stars, figure skaters, concert violinists, gold medal winners, world-class golfers. You read about these kids, how Wayne Gretsky's father had him practice his stick-work on the flooded and frozen back yard every night, the mothers devoting their lives to their figure-skating daughters. And many sons and daughters do follow in the footsteps of their parents and become exactly what the parent wanted. Second and third generations of lawyers and doctors. Jeff Bridges thanking his actor parents as he accepts the Academy Award.

But we would probably have no poets, no inventors, no painters, no explorers, no writers, if all children followed their parents' wishes and dreams.

So some rebellion, some perversity, some risk-taking and rule breaking in adolescence is a good thing, and part of the natural process.

But given all that, and despite your good parenting by example and consistent expectations, your child is in trouble. Your demands and consequences are not working. He's still smoking marijuana. He is still saying he won't go to school. She still comes home in the wee hours of the morning if at all. He never shows up for supper. Even tough-love is failing. And he or she is too young for you to say, "If you want to live that way, my son, you do it on your own dime."

A couple of principles already mentioned can help: some more brain maturity is yet to come. Some intrinsic changes improving the chances for responsibility, ambition, and empathy are on the way. And those current processes of opposition and imitation may be put to work.

The teen has been complaining about and protesting her curfew, the hour she is expected to be home on Saturday night. She argues and argues. In the family therapy session the therapist has told her she may participate in the discussion when she can do so in a civilized and calm fashion. Then he talks with the parents and they discuss the curfew hour. The parents come up with "eleven p.m. unless it is a special event and planned for ahead of time." The therapist then turns to the teenager and says, "Okay. It's your turn to offer an opinion and to negotiate. What do you think?" Invariably the child becomes flustered, seems a little confused, may even mutter something like, "I don't know. It's up to them. Whatever."

Though she has been demanding a say, demanding more, protesting as matter of habit, the moment she is given an opportunity to voice her own opinion, or make her own decision, she retreats. As all citizens of democracies know, it is easier to be in opposition than to actually govern. And for a teen, taking the stance of opposition is much easier than actually making a decision and thus assuming responsibility. Sometimes as a parent you can use that fact.

The fourteen year-old son of a single mother announced that he was no longer attending school. The mother said, "Okay, fair enough. It's up to you. You decide how you want to spend the day. I have to go to work."

The boy says, "But I don't want to go to school."

The mother says, "Okay." And goes back to her coffee.

The dialogue continues for a while, with the mother being careful to place the decision squarely with the boy, and not say anything that would engender that very comfortable position of opposition. Eventually the boy decides to go to school.

There are times you must make the decision for your teen. Then there are times it is wiser to encourage him to make the decision, but if you are doing this you have to be very careful to not provoke the oppositional position.

So if the basics are covered: She is on birth control pills; he is not doing drugs in the house; he or she is attending some kind of school or program or working; they are not stealing; then it can be wise at times to bend like the willow, to not take on, head first, a fight you will lose. You might decide to allow the unsavoury love affair to play out, to ignore the excessive marijuana use for now. Knowing these are battles you will lose, and knowing that your intervention could provoke the opposite result to the one you hoped for, it is sometimes wise to make a strategic retreat. "Retreat" may not be the right word here. "Opting out of this particular conflict because it is not winnable" may be a better way of expressing it.

Sometimes saying to a teen, "It's up to you. You decide." is the best strategy. And then accept the decision, for which your son or daughter must also accept the consequences.

"Okay, you want to quit school, it's up to you. But I will expect you to be paying room and board."

Workarounds require a lot of thought, much flexibility, and some creativity. It might be reasonable for your teen to live with her aunt for a semester, and meet you for dinner once a week. It might be the right thing for your 15 year-old to drop out of school and go to work with his uncle.

One columnist gave in to his son's request to not go to school but insisted they watch movies together and discuss them afterwards. This got the boy through a difficult phase, forged a relationship with his father and provided alternative education.

When your 13 year-old develops a romantic interest in the 19 year-old dropout living next door, it is time to intervene. When your 17 year-old seems to be taking a romantic interest in the 26 year-old high school drop-out part-time drug dealer on probation, it may be time to abide, to ensure she is taking birth control pills, and be ready to pick up the pieces. If you fiercely oppose this one you will probably provoke an elopement.

These are the questions to ask:

Are the basics covered: safety, no criminal activity, no pregnancy, no serious addiction?

Is it a fight I can win if tackled head on? Or are my interventions provoking the exact opposite of what I would like?

If you are unlikely to win the battle head on, think up some other strategy.

Remember the teenager's natural oppositional response and either avoid it, or use it.

VI. Is Something wrong with my teenager?

Mental illnesses that may begin in adolescence can express themselves as despair, sadness, fear, avoidance, anger, withdrawal, and strange symptoms in an otherwise well behaved teen, or as a range of bad, impulsive, strange behaviours that are difficult to distinguish from normal adolescent behaviour except for their persistence and the fact that they are not responding to good parenting. These are:

Bipolar Disorder

Depression

ADHD and ADD

Anxiety Disorder and OCD

Schizophrenia

Depression and Bipolar Disorder

There are some treatable mental or psychiatric illnesses that might be either contributing to your teen's difficulties or causing them. Some of these illnesses, notably bipolar disorder, fairly clearly defined in adulthood, can be difficult to diagnose in adolescence: Teens by definition and developmental phase can be of labile mood, highly reactive, anger easily, retreat quickly, misinterpret easily, daydream in school, misplace their loyalties, and latch onto marginal philosophies and world views. They are also very context dependent. As one mother expressed it:

"From my kitchen window I can see the school bus arrive and let off my daughter and two of her friends. When the bus pulls out they stand around for a good twenty minutes, gossiping, laughing, talking. Then the two friends go off to their homes and my daughter turns to walk up the driveway to our house. And in the driveway I can watch her assume THE ATTITUDE."

"THE ATTITUDE" is that world-weary, sulky, unhappy, petulant expression reserved for parents. Some parents, having either read about bipolar disorder or having a family member diagnosed thus, perceive such behaviour as "she's happy one minute and depressed or angry the next" and possibly evidence of bipolar disorder. But what is described above is simply context dependent behaviour. This child has the capacity for happiness and sadness and irritability. What she experiences and what emotions she displays depend on her context. To move too quickly to an assumption of a bipolar disorder has three major drawbacks:

1. The abrogation of responsibility implied by having a disease causing the bad behaviour. A sort of "never guilty by reason of insanity" plea.

2. The initiation of treatment with medication that is far from simple or benign.

3. The potential of interpreting all future discomfort and problems as symptoms of bipolar disease.

But manic-depressive disorder (bipolar disorder) and depression can begin in adolescence. Unfortunately, the physiological markers for depression and bipolar illness in adults do not hold as well for adolescents: these are sleep disturbance, appetite loss, weight loss, loss of libido, decrease in interest, concentration, energy, and mood.

And adolescent self-reporting is not reliable. It is not unusual for an adolescent to say, "I'm always depressed." when clearly she is not, for you have observed her spend an hour happily talking and laughing with a friend. For an adolescent "always" and "forever" may refer to some small increment of time beyond this moment. "Almost nobody" can refer to 2 out of 5. (As in "almost none of my friends smoke marijuana") "Almost never" can refer to 3 out of 5. (As in "I almost never skip classes"). The statement "I was depressed all weekend." might exclude hours on the phone, chatting on ICQ or MSN, dancing at the party. And phrases such as "I want to die." or "I might as well be dead." or "I'm thinking of killing myself." can refer to the momentary displeasure experienced when zits erupt, when the boyfriend does not phone, when one is asked to take out the garbage, or when the school project is overdue.

Parental reporting is mostly from one context and may reflect the child's relationship with his parents rather than something intrinsically wrong in the child's head.

But **pervasive, persistent, and not context bound, irritability, social withdrawal, sleep disturbance, and low mood** may be signs of a true clinical or treatable depression. Further warning signs that your child's behaviour could be explained as products of this illness are:

1. A strong family history of mood disorders.

2. A genuine hypo-manic or manic episode consisting of very high energy, rapid speech, sleeplessness (not needing sleep), very labile or excessively happy mood, fits of giggling, overconfidence, extreme impulsivity, grandiosity, and delusional thinking. (Use of amphetamine drugs such as Crystal Meth can cause the same symptoms, or even trigger a manic episode in someone predisposed to this illness)

3. A persistent depressive mood that is **not** context dependent and not the result of a recent disappointment or loss. This depressed mood may be associated with physiological changes such as sleep disturbance (especially early morning wakening), loss of appetite, change of menstrual pattern, loss of energy, and social changes such as withdrawal from friends as well as school. (A common pattern of withdrawal from school but not from friends is usually not a signal of depression but of a different problem such as drug use, bullying, academic difficulties, or simple adolescent avoidance of work or any activity that does not provide immediate gratification.)

Talk with your family doctor, and get a referral to a child/adolescent psychiatrist to help sort this out.

ADD and ADHD

Both Attention Deficit Disorder and Attention Deficit Hyperactivity Disorder are common contributors to outrageous adolescent behaviour. Untreated, a boy with ADHD is far more likely to drop out of school, use drugs, become addicted, steal, engage in risky behaviour, and spend time in jail, than either a boy without ADHD or a boy with ADHD who is receiving treatment.

Neither ADD nor ADHD arise in adolescence but there are reasons these two problems might have been missed in childhood. A boy with ADHD might have avoided diagnosis and treatment with medication because he was able to attend small classes with very good teachers, and because he received consistent strong parenting, and because he was smart enough to always stop short of failing, or hitting, or jumping out of his window. Or perhaps the diagnosis was made but the boy's parents were reluctant to put their son on stimulant medication.

A girl with ADD may not have been diagnosed in childhood, in elementary school, because she was always polite and pleasant and likeable, if a little dreamy and inattentive. But this short attention span, this distractibility, combined with new freedoms and new hormones, can quickly lead to misadventure in adolescence.

The main problem posed by ADHD and ADD is acting and reacting without thinking, along with school failure or truancy. Adolescents are already prone to acting and reacting without thinking. Add ADHD or ADD to the mix and the stage is set for high-risk behaviour.

It may be useful to comment on how the normal human brain works. When confronted by a stimulus, a provocative event, such as a fresh donut, being bumped in the hallway, a beautiful woman, a cute boy, should electrodes be implanted in our brains, they would show activity in the motor cortex. We are about to reach for the donut, punch back in the hallway, move toward the attractive man or woman. And then other parts of the brain activate – the memory, judgment, assessment areas - and we (our brains, at least) reconsider this action and quell the activity in the motor cortex - all before we have actually moved or even given it conscious thought. It is this latter brain activity that is missing with ADD and ADHD, the ability to **inhibit** a sequence of brain and motor events that has already been initiated by the stimulus. As Bart Simpson once said, "I don't know why I did it. I know I shouldn't have done it, and I know I'll do it again."

Normally a child does something he shouldn't and suffers consequences. Perhaps he has to do it twice and suffer the consequences twice before learning to inhibit that particular behaviour. But a child with ADD/ADHD doesn't seem to learn from consequences. He has reacted before his brain has a chance to consider outcome. Unfortunately this can lead to repeated bad behaviour, repeated consequences, always being in trouble, always on the wrong side of teachers and parents, calling up the need for more defiance, more defensive and offensive attitude, and a "Who cares!" position, and of course, a destination of very early pregnancy, or criminal record, and/or addiction.

There is always controversy about ADHD, and ADD. Is it a true illness? Or is this just boy behaviour in the context of a feminised school system that expects a quiet, polite demeanour for long periods of time, a system with zero tolerance for snow ball fights, spit balls, and any other form of aggression, playful or otherwise? Should we be drugging our kids to help the teachers? About once per year in each North American Sunday paper there appears a lengthy article entitled: "Are we overmedicating our children?"

In my elementary school days I was a mostly good kid, academically and athletically successful, the son of a school principal. I was often one of only two kids let out for grade six recesses, having finished all the required math questions. Nonetheless, I was the one somehow chosen in my grade two class to fight the grade three bully, with the other kids standing in a circle cheering me on. And again I was the one to fight for and rescue my younger brother being unfairly targeted during a snowball fight a few years later. There would be zero tolerance for this in today's schools.

Ah, the good old days. I suspect this kind of boy play is important. We learned to compete aggressively, within rules we designed ourselves and deemed fair, and we corrected those who broke the rules. There is a way to conduct a snowball fight, and the kid who decides to throw ice balls or rocks or get too close is quickly corrected.

Today's schools have limited such learning opportunities, for better or for worse. Boys are quick to be sent to the principal's office and suspended, today, for something that might have been forgiven as "roughhousing" a few decades ago. So perhaps the expectations of some of our elementary schools are a bit unrealistic. Should 10 year-old boys be expected to sit quietly for 45 minutes and to never engage in teasing or rough play? In the rest of the animal kingdom it is this kind of competitive, and sometimes aggressive, play that prepares cubs and puppies for life as adults.

Nonetheless, severe ADHD seems to be, by self-evidence, an intrinsic disorder. The child's or teen's motor is running at a high RPM no matter the context. He can't sit still for even a few minutes. He can't hold a thought or focus for more than a second or two. He always reacts without thinking. He appears to have no working memory – that is, the ability to hold in his mind the sequence of actions required to arrive at a goal. While engaging in part three of the process he has forgotten part two. And pretty soon some noise or sight or thought will distract him altogether.

Milder ADD and ADHD is not so self-evidentially a disorder of the brain. In many circumstances and contexts the child behaves well. It is the teacher reporting difficult behaviour, and perhaps the teacher's expectations are too - what might the word be? - Too high, too feminine, too conservative? Such a child as this raises the questions alluded to above.

But a practical approach to this problem of perception and definition of ADD and ADHD is as follows:

Our school systems are what they are. Resources are limited. It is unlikely that each child can receive the degree of one-on-one supervision and organized activity that a boy with ADHD might require, whether or not that ADHD is a disease or just an extension of boy-ness. And it is clearly better for a child to have academic and social success than not to have these. It was once possible for a boy to drop out of school before grade seven and work on the farm with his dad or his uncle. Even the very small number of boys who still have that opportunity in rural communities will need literacy, computer, mechanical, and bookkeeping skills on today's farm.

Academic AND social failure in childhood is a prescription for a marginal life in adulthood. If medication is required to achieve this success, then it is a very small price to pay.

So it is possible that ADHD or ADD is contributing to your son's or daughter's difficult behaviour in adolescence. The signs that this might be the case include some evidence of ADHD/ADD in childhood, a predilection to alcohol and drugs, especially impulsive and thoughtless risky behaviour, speaking without thought, very quickly regressing to the language and attitude of a two year-old, repeatedly getting into trouble despite his or her wish to not do so, and despite your best efforts as a parent. (When asked if they would like to be in less trouble, they almost all say, "Yes". And when asked if taking a pill once per day would help keep them out of trouble and do better at school, they almost all are happy to take that pill. They do not want to fail at school and be yelled at by parents.)

The dilemma posed for treating ADHD in adolescence is the not uncommon possibility that your teen will misuse the medication prescribed: sell it to his friends, mix it dangerously with Crystal Meth or Ecstasy, or crush it and snort it, or even overdose on it to "get high".

Nonetheless, if the parents adequately supervise the administration of the medication, and the child discovers that, indeed, he does better at school and gets in trouble less often, then it is well worth ensuring adequate supervised treatment. A good nine out of ten adolescents taking a stimulant medication for ADD or ADHD are happy taking it to do better in school, and not be yelled at so often by mom and dad. There is always that one out of ten who would like "his old self back" when he had more fun, but this may have more to do with parenting.

ADD (ADHD without the Hyperactivity), more common in girls than ADHD (though both are more common in boys) may go undetected through elementary school. This might be a nice child, quiet, non-disruptive, polite, happy, simply a child who does not perform well, does poorly in her work, doesn't get it finished, day dreams and drifts. She has friends. She is likeable. The teachers will pass her from one grade to the next. Her struggles to pay attention, to hold a working memory, her failing grades, may not pose a major problem until her teens. By then she will have fallen behind her peers, lost some of her friends, and been unsuccessful in most things she tries. Her self-esteem will suffer, and now that she is a young woman, she can drift into, or be led into, activities she is not ready for. An adolescent girl with ADD is at risk of failing and dropping out of school, not gaining other useful skills, following her fleeting whims, shop-lifting unsuccessfully, and getting pregnant. Most such teenagers would like to do better at school, would like to drift into trouble less often, would like things to be calmer at home, and to get along with their parents better.

The same precautions with regard to misuse of medication apply to the girls as well as the boys.

But apart from these precautions, the most gratifying aspect of treating ADD and ADHD is the prospect of instant improvement. The pills prescribed (Ritalin, Dexedrine and related drugs) usually work and usually work immediately. Both the child and the people around her may notice a difference right away, an improvement in paying attention in class, a decrease in impulsivity, an ability to refrain from saying the first thing that comes to mind, a new ability to curb petulant and child-like responses, better marks right away. You may suddenly have a polite, helpful, and mostly dependable child on your hands. If the medication doesn't help or causes a paradoxical effect this usually means the diagnosis was wrong and the medication can be simply stopped with no adverse effect.

Anxiety Disorder and Obsessive Compulsive Disorder

An anxiety disorder with panic attacks, and an obsessive-compulsive disorder can arise in the teen years, though pre-teen anxieties and phobias may have preceded it. Usually, this does not occur in an out-of-control badly behaved child. Usually this develops in an otherwise well behaved, sometimes too well behaved child.

But it may be hidden from you. The child who must check things twice then thrice, who must count things, must organize things, who must spell in his mind the words just spoken, who must eat food in a certain order, may not tell you this is happening. But his marks are falling, he is having trouble getting to sleep, and he feels sick to the stomach each school morning. His natural adolescent self-consciousness may increase to a feeling that his peers are always looking at him, and that they find him wanting in some way. She may feel she is being judged all the time: her appearance, her intelligence, her morality. She spends hours trying and failing to get her hair just right. He spends hours in the shower. He may refuse school. He retreats into video games. She retreats into MSN, Facebook and SIMS.

A friend calls to go hang out at the mall, or to skateboard, but the teen begs off. They fall into a pattern of being up all night (on video games or chat rooms) and asleep during the day. At this point they might deny feeling any anxiety, because they don't go anywhere that might provoke it.

Occasionally an anxiety disorder lies behind what otherwise seems to be obstinate, defiant behaviour, moodiness and school refusal. The boy won't go to school. He says because he "just doesn't want to". He simply, "Doesn't like school." He is not going to admit to fear or anxiety. At home he is surly, defiant. He has quit sports. He claims he'd rather play video games, or he was too late to sign up for basketball this year anyway.

He is now comfortable and without symptoms, sleeping in until noon, sometimes hooking up with a fellow social isolate, and otherwise honing his video game skills. If he does actually go out and party with friends, he finds his anxiety can be alleviated with copious amounts of alcohol. And then he might find, that though his mornings are still lousy, daily use, and especially regular evening use of marijuana alleviates some of his anxiety and helps him sleep. He won't want to quit using because it "makes me feel better."

A strong family history of anxiety or mood disorders is often present.

This is a very treatable condition. (Though much more difficult when alcohol and marijuana dependence is involved) It usually responds well to a combination of family therapy, some individual counselling, and medication. The family therapy component is important because, as mentioned above, this teenager is quite comfortable sleeping till noon or three in the afternoon, then sitting on the computer until four in the morning, with a few breaks for foraging in the refrigerator, avoiding the rest of the family. And the family therapy component will be essential if the anxiety disorder is compounded by excessive alcohol use and self-medicating with marijuana.

You will need help finding the right balance of accommodation, expectations, and treatment. When to push, when to encourage, and when to accommodate.

Schizophrenia

The common age of onset of this most devastating of mental illnesses is between 18 and 24, but it can begin as early as 13 or 14. The earlier the onset the poorer the prognosis. The more insidious the onset the poorer the prognosis. An acute psychotic episode at age 21 is better than a slowly progressing psychotic illness with earlier onset. But we do now have medications that can control the more severe symptoms, and the sooner treatment is received the better the prognosis. It is simply not a good thing to spend any great length of time interpreting the world and life around you in a delusional fashion, especially during those years of your life in which your job is to figure out how everything fits together.

We still don't really understand this illness, though it has been with us since recorded history, in all cultures, at about the same rate: one in one hundred people. Though the underlying physiological causes may be the same, the expression of the illness is modulated with the times, the technologies, the cultural beliefs. In the 1950's it was not uncommon for someone developing schizophrenia to decide X-Rays, or radio waves were controlling him, though that would not be the case two hundred years before. Then it would more likely be God or one of his emissaries, or Satan. But now it might be digital implants, or something unnamed the CIA is working on.

The role of marijuana is being studied. Some researchers believe it plays a causative role. But certainly regular marijuana use can begin as self-medicating and end up contributing to, or even precipitating, that first psychotic episode in a vulnerable teenager.

Schizophrenia is too complex an illness to discuss at any length in this book. There are many other resources to turn to. For a truthful overview:

"Schizophrenia: Medicine's Mystery, Society's Shame" – Marvin Ross, Bridgeross Communications.

For one way of understanding the development and symptoms of the illness:

"Schizophrenia in Focus" – David Dawson, Heather Blum, Gianpero Bartolucci – Human Sciences Press.

For what you can do as parents:

"Surviving Schizophrenia" - Fuller Torrey

Schizophrenia is seldom diagnosed right away. This because even psychiatrists are reluctant to apply this most distressing of labels to a young boy or girl, and because the early symptoms can mimic depression and anxiety or OCD, and because the sufferer is always reluctant to reveal the full extent of his strange experiences.

But here are some of the early indicators, the observations that should compel you to request a referral to a psychiatrist:

His or her depression is persistent, causing social withdrawal, avoidance of peers, and his mood is not so much sad as blunt, vague. His eyes are often puzzled and perplexed. He communicates less and less, and when he does it is often in cryptic remarks. He sleeps during the day and is awake at night, spending some of that time not playing video games but sitting in silence.

She seems now inordinately fascinated by cults and strange interpretations of human life and God. Your family is not particularly religious but he has taken to reading passages in the bible. Or your family is religious but his take on it is strange and fanatical. He now prefers the blinds in his room closed all day as well as all night.

He has developed some odd social quirks not present before; he has lost the spontaneous fluid facial and hand movements of his childhood.

Like his peers he has over-indulged with alcohol, but then done some especially bizarre thing, something difficult to explain and out-of-character. (carved an initial on his chest, walked to city hall naked, jumped from the train trestle after professing a religious belief, told you he is being hunted by the FBI).

You know she suffers from anxiety, and has some OCD traits, but now her obsessions have taken on an other-worldly quality, and the level of distress she experiences when she cannot complete a compulsion is extreme. As if she truly believes that if she doesn't repeat that magic word exactly ten times in her head, or prays for 15 minutes, her parents will die in a car accident.

He or she has said odd things to you, and you have let them slide; perhaps you have interpreted them, seen them as just adolescent craziness. But looking back, if you take them at face value, they indicate quite a distorted world-view.

That feeling he had, that at school, his peers, people he knows, were often looking at him and talking about him in a negative way, has spread to strangers in the mall, and even people in automobiles driving by. He believes they are all judging him, and talking about him. He doesn't tell you that he can hear them talking about him. When you ask this he is avoidant and vague.

He seems to be puzzling about everything, trying to work out patterns. He writes some of this down. Her journaling makes references to God and Love and Hate with some numbers and 'plus' and 'equal' signs.

He has done a couple of very odd things and you cannot get an explanation from him and you have not been able to figure out an explanation that would be both plausible and sane.

His dependence on you has become extreme and conflicted. He is angry with you, blaming you for everything, but at the same time his social development seems frozen at age 13 though now he is 17.

The seventeen year-old boy ran along a school roof, spread his arms and jumped. He landed on a second roof twenty feet below, causing a broken bone or two, bruising and bleeding. A 'tox' screen done in the emergency room did not reveal any mind-altering substances. After recovering from his physical injuries it turned out he had sufficient symptoms of schizophrenia to make that diagnosis. But his jump remained a puzzle. He had not known about that second roof and had expected the fall to be more like an eighty-foot drop. But he wasn't trying to kill himself. He had not been suicidal. It wasn't until his illness had been treated and a year had passed that he told us he jumped because a voice told him to do this in order to save the world from an evil force.

Because this may be an unfolding illness, and because the sufferer will not tell you or the family doctor or the psychiatrist the extent of his abnormal experiences and thoughts right away, this teenager should be seeing, with parents, the family doctor or a psychiatrist on a regular basis to monitor and assess over a period of time.

VII. FAQs

- **Cars**
- **Shoplifting & Other Stealing**
- **Cutting and Self-mutilation**
- **Preoccupations with the morbid**
- **Anorexia & Bulimia**
- **Sex & Pregnancy**
- **Sexual orientation and Gender Identity**
- **Drugs and Alcohol**

Cars (and boats, motorcycles and snowmobiles)

It is my observation that boys and girls are far more likely to be involved in accidents, sometimes fatal, when driving mother's or father's car or a car that has been given to them, than when driving a car they actually worked for, paid for, fixed up themselves.

They are simply not as careful with mother's car. A car loaded with girls, talking, laughing, gossiping, putting on makeup, talking on the cell phone, MP3 players on high volume, is not safe. A car loaded with boys egging one another on, drinking beer, burning rubber, is not safe.

They are teenagers. They do not feel mortal or vulnerable. Nothing bad can happen. And they don't care about the car. They don't care about the car because they are deficient in empathy for their parents, and they can't imagine the consequences of an accident.

A teenage boy who worked and saved and bought his own car with his own money, and cleaned the spark plugs, and rebuilt the carburettor, is still immortal and invulnerable, **but he will be careful about what happens to his car**. He will drive more carefully. He will not allow his friends to eat Sloppy Joes in the back seat. He might even check the oil and washer fluid on occasion.

Ideally then, the teenager should not have access to a car until and unless he or she can buy or build her own. A compromise solution is to make sure the teen has paid for, worked for, in some partial way at least, the privilege of having access to a car.

At the very least, to keep your teen from becoming tragic front-page news, make sure you insist that access to a family car is a privilege earned by a sustained demonstration of responsibility. And certainly, one episode of reckless behaviour while driving a car should mean your teen is denied driving privileges for at least six months.

It is the same with boats, motorcycles, and snowmobiles. If they worked for it, paid for it, purchased it themselves using their own hard-earned money they will take better care of it, and this means they are less likely to have fatal accidents in it or on it.

A few years ago in Ontario a boy was released from a juvenile detention facility, a youth centre. That very night he asked his father for the keys to dad's Cadillac. These were given to him. At two AM the next morning this boy and his three passengers died in a "single car accident on a country road".

Shoplifting

There would appear to be three kinds of adolescent shoplifting. The first kind is simply boundary testing, thrill seeking, with peer encouragement - doing something naughty. The object stolen often does not make sense. A blouse that does not fit, lipstick not used. It is the simple **possibility** of shoplifting and peer encouragement that motivates the action, not the need or want of an object. Fortunately, most teens, having experienced the anxiety, and then the guilt and possible shame of the behaviour, will not bother doing it again. A few will enjoy the thrill and continue doing it until caught.

Then there is shoplifting of things wanted: a coveted blouse, the hottest CD, a pair of hundred dollar jeans. This is an adolescent who feels deprived and entitled. There may be no real basis for these feelings. They may simply be remnants of childhood. Peers may encourage and rationalize these feelings. Or, the teen's parents might be paying a little less attention during a difficult time in their lives – a divorce, a dying grandparent. Or this teen, without other means of achieving acceptance, membership, self-esteem, competency, needs to show off to her peers. Left unchecked, shoplifting can become a regular weekend activity for a group of teens.

And finally, shoplifting can be more specifically criminal: The theft of articles to be turned into cash to buy drugs.

No matter the nature of the shoplifting and other theft, the first necessary parental responses are the same.

Of course, the parents must first be alert to the possibility of stealing. We are all primed to accept the most facile and illogical explanations from our children. We want to believe them.

> *A father says, "Where'd that new X-Box come from?" And the boy answers, "I bought it from Kyle with my birthday money." The father is about to say, "But an X-Box must be worth a hundred bucks and your birthday was six* months ago *and your grandparents only gave you thirty dollars....." but he doesn't. He wants to believe his son.*

> *The mother says, "I don't remember seeing those jeans before." And the girl says, "They belong to Alison. She let me borrow them." And the mother is about to say, "But Alison is two sizes smaller than you." But she doesn't. She wants to believe.*

As serious a matter as stealing is, we needn't see shoplifting as a catastrophe. It does not mean your child is a criminal in the making. He or she is deficient in the frontal lobe department, but this is a developmental phase. He still has a few more years to develop empathy, guilt, and the ability to weigh the likely cost versus benefit of an action. But you do need to act. If your child has not been caught you may try to deal with the problem within the home. Not with questions, courtroom drama, the pulling of hair, but simply with the purloined articles being returned and the child punished. Along with a warning that if the behaviour repeats, the store in question will be informed, and encouraged to lay charges. Yes. When it comes to stealing, the police, the court, the probation officers are your friends.

This action alone should end the first variety of shoplifting discussed above. Deep in her heart she may be grateful she was caught before her peers managed to talk her into bigger and more risky heists.

For the second kind of shoplifting, once the bad behaviour has been punished, it would be reasonable for the parents to look more closely. Perhaps the child is missing the parental attention she needs. Perhaps she or he needs more structure, more guidance, more control. Perhaps she or he needs to be directed away from current peers and toward supervised peer activities in which skills and competence are gained. Perhaps she needs a part-time job.

Severe and swift action needs to be taken if the third kind of shoplifting is occurring. Both the stealing and the drug use need to be addressed. You try to handle it within the home. But if your brand of tough love is not working, do not hesitate to use community resources. Your local police may have a specific division for this, or a "community officer", or the town is small enough that you personally know one of the Sergeants.

There are some common patterns to other types of stealing. As mentioned before, typically when the teenage boy steals it is to buy drugs. When the teenage girl steals it is just as likely for toys, trinkets, gifts to friends. Assume drug use when your boy steals. Assume either drug use or a child desperate to impress her friends when your daughter steals.

In-home stealing follows the pattern of: loose change left on the counter, the change jar on top the refrigerator, rifling in wallets and purses, objects that can be easily sold: CD's, DVD's, electronics, cameras, tools, jewellery. (The Blue-Ray player dies and you go looking for the DVD player you put on the shelf and it's gone, along with your tool kit). Then come credit cards, and ATM cards, and then the forging of cheques to be cashed at the Money Mart. When a neighbour calls to tell you he thinks your boy took his new twelve-megapixel Nikon, do not get defensive. And do not take your son's denial as any kind of Gospel truth, even if he says, "I swear to God." Investigate dispassionately.

When objects disappear in a household visited by 12 to 19 year-olds you might use some demographic profiling to ascertain the culprit. The poltergeist phenomenon is interesting. Though it may provide a good vehicle for a horror movie, the reality always consists of things moved, or set in motion, by someone between the ages of 12 and 19.

Your house is neither a democracy nor a court of law. When things or money go missing, and a human between the ages of 12 and 20 lives in your home, he is guilty until proved innocent. Not that the first time this happens you can't approach it cautiously, tentatively, but if on that rare occasion when it turns out your twenty dollar bill actually fell behind the dresser, and your child did not purloin it, you can always demonstrate maturity and apologize.

Stealing needs to be addressed quickly and definitively. Work out a schedule of payback with specific chores. Take away a toy of equal value. Ground for a week. Don't worry about the denials and lying. As mentioned before, having stolen, the boy must lie. The lying is natural if irritating. It is the stealing that needs to be addressed. And the reasons for stealing, if there are any.

If it cannot be dealt with at home successfully, use community resources. With serious stealing and continued stealing, call the police and let the police, the courts, and the probation services help you bring your son or daughter under control. Unless it is stopped, it does not get better. If it is not stopped it will grow. It will follow a predictable pattern of desensitisation: the teen's thefts will grow in size, audacity and risk, as he gets more comfortable with his criminal activities. Individual counselling will not help. But the whole family attending a counsellor might help develop an action plan with which you can be comfortable.

Cutting & Self-mutilation

This must be one of the more perplexing behaviours confronting the parents of young teens today. Why on earth would your 13 year-old sit in her room and deftly scratch at her arm with a sharp object? Usually the cuts are limited to the wrist area and barely break the surface of the skin, but they can extend to thighs and upper arms, and occasionally go deep enough to cause scarring.

If you ask your teen why she is doing this she will tell you "It feels better", or "It takes away the pain." This is, of course, universally true. A physical injury will distract the mind from emotional pain, obsessions or preoccupations. So she is probably telling the truth, at least in so far as she understands it. But her explanation is very limited and unhelpful.

Only rarely is such cutting caused by depression, and seldom is it related in any way to that which we tend to call, "a suicide attempt." Usually it is part of a group pattern. That is, the teen who cuts usually knows another teen who cuts. Cutting is often peer-sanctioned behaviour. This sanctioning or enabling of cutting may also reach your teen via MSN gossip or certain "alternative life-style" web sites.

Usually such behaviour follows some episode of distress caused by peer rejection, boyfriend rejection, hurtful comments made vocally or via MSN, Facebook, and text messaging, or simply from the confusion and regret that itself follows from having gotten into something, or done something regrettable the last few days (sex, drugs, alcohol, meanness, theft, violence). It can result from simple anguished confusion about sex, drugs, and rock and roll – meaning about the complex, sometimes incredibly naïve and primitive relationships in which she is entangled with her peers.

Always, cutting is a message to parents that your child is overwhelmed, over-her-head, out-of-her depth – that her social, sexual, or other activities are beyond her maturity – that she does not yet have the capacity to respond to these kinds of emotional hurts, confusions, expectations, in a more reasonable fashion. Your child is saying to you: **"I can't handle what's going on. Please help me and make me feel safe."**

She is not asking this directly. Such a direct request would conflict with her equally strong wish for independence, and her need to maintain an illusion of her own maturity.

Knowing this, how should parents respond?

In a sense, the specific causes of the feeling of being overwhelmed are not (usually) important. They are, and must be, part of growing up: rejections, academic struggles, peer nastiness, social and sexual confusion, infatuation and love, disappointment and loss. (Though of course, a parent must always be on the alert for bullying and sexual abuse) The problem is, this child is not yet ready to face the life issues confronting her, at least not on her own. So at this point she needs:

- Respite from these life issues.
- To learn that cutting is not an appropriate response.
- To learn there are other ways of dealing with these issues.

To satisfy all three needs, the child's parents should do the following:

After talking it through together, and realizing that no matter the issues facing this teen, and doing what is advised is both safe and practical, they should formally meet with their teen and say this to her:

"We love you, and we are here for you. We are always ready to listen to your problems and help you. But cutting and other forms of self-mutilation will not be tolerated in this household. You are hereby grounded for two weeks, and should you cut again you will be grounded for one month. Your grounding means that you will attend school, attend any other adult supervised activities, spend time with us, do your homework, sleep, but otherwise have no unsupervised activities with your peers, including boyfriends, no telephone time, no cell phone, no internet, and no MSN."

The child is likely to respond with, "But that won't make me happy." Or words to that effect, but as we know, this child is a child and does not have the judgement to know what will and what will not give her some peace of mind. She may pout or show temper. But you are making her safe, and you will find that your daughter is once again smiling within 24 or 48 hours.

As in all such matters, deep in their hearts they want to feel safe; they want to have their parents keep them safe, and, though they won't admit it, the two weeks sans cell phone, MSN, and chat rooms, will relieve them of the terrible stress of interminable social negotiation.

Of course, words will not suffice. Parents must be prepared to act. And if MSN or Internet chat rooms or cell phone usage has been a major culprit, these should be limited and monitored after the two-week hiatus.

Many parents find it difficult to respond in the manner suggested above. These difficulties arise from a number of sources:

1. Practical: single working parent unable to supervise a complete two-week grounding or lock down.

2. Over identification: remembering your own hurts and confusions as a teen.

3. Guilt: A feeling that your teen is behaving in this way because of you, because you took her away from her father, because you have to work, because you are pre-occupied by your own problems.

4. Love: you desperately want to make her happy.

The first problem is difficult, but stopping this behaviour (cutting) early on is important, so use your resources: parents, ex-spouse, uncles, aunts, friends, holiday time.

The second problem is common with today's small families and busy parent(s). In some ways the problem is not that we pay too little attention to our adolescents, but too much. This teen is a work-in-progress. She is not you. You are not her. You are an adult with a full adult life. Your job is to provide the environment in which your teen can grow safely into adulthood.

Teenagers slip into bad behaviour. It is not your fault. Even if a great deal of your teen's confusion can be traced to your marital strife, depression, separation, absences, your guilt will not help. More than ever she needs a confident parent at her side.

Of course you would like to see your child happy, smiling, successful. But as an adult you know there is a vast difference between the momentary glee that comes from doing what you please, getting away with something, satisfying a craving, and the happiness that comes from a sense of accomplishment within a loving and safe environment. You don't need to help her achieve momentary glee. That is something about which most teens do not need instruction. Your job is to provide an environment within which she can gain skills, confidence, self-assurance, and a sense of being both loved and safe.

So tell her this, and act upon your words, without guilt or doubt:

"We love you, and we are here for you. We are always ready to listen to your problems and help you. But cutting and other forms of self-mutilation will not be tolerated in this household. You are hereby grounded for two weeks, and should you cut again you will be grounded for one month. Your grounding means that you will attend school, attend any other supervised activities, spend time with us, do your homework, sleep, but otherwise have no unsupervised activities with your peers, including boyfriends, no telephone time, no cell phone, no internet, and no MSN."

Most teens who cut are, if anything, over-involved socially, at least in unsupervised social activities with peers, or a single boyfriend or girlfriend, or an ex-boyfriend plus his new girlfriend, who was once her best friend. But occasionally, self-mutilation does signify a more serious problem, such as clinical depression, anxiety or psychosis. Extreme social withdrawal, or an absence of friends of any kind (virtual or real), along with cutting, may indicate a true (or clinical) depression is developing. And if the cutting is, in it's manner and severity, and choice of instrument, particularly bizarre, and coupled with obsessions and/or compulsive behaviours, this may indicate a developing psychotic illness. In these situations you should have your child referred to a child psychiatrist and attend with her. While waiting for the appointment you might still enact the advice given above.

Preoccupations with the Morbid

666 had recently passed when I began this writing. June 6, 2006. A local cemetery was desecrated by a small group of teens, tombstones pushed over in the night. A month later a seventeen year-old boy confesses, at the insistence of his mother. The newspaper reports that the seventeen year-old, with his fourteen year-old girlfriend and a few other teens, were looking for a Devil's Day party at the cemetery. In his explanation, the newspaper reports, he claims some of the tombstones were already knocked over. "We just finished the job. It was a rush. We were just having fun. Some of us had the group work on them together because they were so big. It was something to do."

The newspaper then reports that the seventeen year-old is "into Punk, Goth, Thrash and Heavy Metal. He likes Korn, Tool, Disturbed, Slipknot and Mudvayne." This is what caught my eye. Why not be "into" Beethoven's early quartets or post-Maharaja Beatles? I know it's a silly question. If it doesn't disturb and shock us, what's the point?

A couple of times a month a parent arrives in my office with a teen in tow, the teen sporting dyed black straightened hair, heavy black eye shadow, enhanced black eye lashes, black or violet finger nails, metal piercing eyebrows, lip and tongue, chains and dog collars, black shirt and ripped black pants. "I'm into Goth," they say. "I like the style. I'm expressing myself." They name bands like the few mentioned above. They write morbid poetry. The mother sitting beside this Alien is dressed in twenty-first century suburban.

I understand this child's need to individuate, to use her two methods of opposition and imitation to accomplish this. I

125

understand how Thrash Metal music and Zombie clothing will garner the required reaction from parents.

The parents of these children are often very understanding and tolerant. Perhaps too understanding. Perhaps that is why the kid has to push it so far. (I can see my own daughter dressing like this for a party, but I think I would have insisted on human clothing for an appointment with the doctor.)

But why the preoccupation with death, limbo, Satan, the Anti-Christ, blood, rituals, killing, and dismemberment? Why not choose equally outrageous styles and costumes and music that are not so morbid?

It is true that Goth and blood, rage, and primitive rituals will shock the parents more, but there may be another reason. Though the adolescent behaves as if invulnerable, and immortal, he is experiencing **intimations of mortality**. He has just left a phase in life when he was protected, invulnerable, special; when the sun always came up in the morning and life was eternal. Now he's beginning to understand that he too has a body of cells and blood vessels with a limited life span, that life brings many questions with no answers. He is now conscious of himself. He is facing large and very frightening questions.

So preoccupation with Goth Culture may satisfy two anxieties. On one hand it can help her individuate; she can oppose and imitate and shock, and engage in that ever-present struggle to define herself while feeling that she belongs to a group. At the same time she can ameliorate her real fears by making them her own, her hobbies, caricatures of the real thing, pretend-mortality and pretend-death. She can deal with the growing anxiety caused by her nascent awareness of mortality and vulnerability by turning it into a game, a little drama, a costume party, by simply proclaiming that she is "into Goth or Zombies or Vampires".

What can a parent do?

126

Much horrible music and outrageous dress is harmless. It can be one of the more benign ways of imitating and opposing and individuating. She will grow out of such tastes and needs. In extreme form (cutting, self-mutilation, pushing over tombstones, suicide pacts, career limiting tattoos) it is not benign.

Most of the parents of Goth teens I see have been all too understanding. The child has to push the boundary of taste and outrageous behaviour further and further to get a reaction. These tend to be parents who insist on respecting their adolescent's opinions, choice of dress, web site preoccupations, and their choice of adornments. But their adolescent is looking for a reaction, and if he doesn't get one he will push and push. So react. Tell her in no uncertain terms that you don't like tattoos, black eye shadow, the whole morbid Goth thing, that terrible music. Maybe if she knows she's getting the desired reaction for doing that much, she won't have to take it any further.

Monitor the web sites she visits. Don't hesitate to pull the plug on the Internet if you find she is visiting places she shouldn't.

Do your best to get her involved in healthier pursuits, clubs, and alternative groups to join.

If your teen has reached the point of cutting, self-mutilation, vandalism, and career limiting tattoos, it is time to react strongly and definitively. This calls for the end of certain associations, the end of MSN, a period of grounding, and some form of community service or work.

Give them goals; if you can't give them goals, give them hope; if you can't give them hope, **keep them busy**.

Is there a way of helping your teen deal with his real anxieties of mortality and vulnerability, of illness, loss and death, in a healthier manner?

You probably can't get him going to church on a regular basis. You probably can't get her interested in more mainstream (and far more difficult) philosophies and religions. But I wonder if the boy who pushed over the tombstones would have done that, had he:

- Helped bury his pet dog or rabbit and put a marker on the grave and said a few words with Mom standing beside him at least once in his childhood.

- Visited his Grandfather in the hospital and then attended the funeral and burial at his father's side.

- Once a year gone with his family to put flowers on his uncle's grave.

Your teen needs a way of handling his intimations of mortality, his own new awareness of loss, illness, injury, finality, and death. We all need rituals, communal sharing, and periods of solemnity to negotiate the large transitions of life. If you don't belong to an organized religion with established rituals of observance, then try to add some to your family life. The children should go to an uncle's funeral, visit the gravesite. They should be encouraged to develop their own service for the burial of a pet. They should have the opportunity to talk with you about these things.

And, as with all teen issues, if family rituals, observations, logic, reason, discussion, and boundaries don't suffice, keep him busy.

Anorexia and Bulimia

Many years ago a fourteen year-old girl who was refusing to eat was admitted to my care on a psychiatric ward. The first child suffering from Anorexia Nervosa I would treat. Her mother was the Chief Nutritionist of the Provincial Psychiatric Hospital. Interesting, I thought, as I read all I could about the condition. But it might be a coincidence, a happenstance, a small irony.

A couple of months later a second Anorexic girl was admitted under my care. And it turned out her father was the Professor and Chief of Internal Medicine at the University. Now one is an accident, but two is a pattern.

This refusal to eat, this kind of anorexia, appears to be a problem limited to the Western world, predominantly North America. One just doesn't see it happening in large families where food is scarce. In fact, these anorexic girls almost all come from upper-middle class and professional families. Perhaps you can imagine the response of the large family of an itinerant farm worker when the thirteen year old refuses to eat the Taco placed in front of her.

So it is difficult to imagine that it is in some way an intrinsic disease, a brain problem like other mental illnesses. These other illnesses, the ones listed in the section on mental illness, occur at about the same rate in all cultures without regard to social class.

Quite a bit has been made of our preoccupation with the unnatural slimness of fashion models, and how this might be influencing our teenage girls, how it might be contributing to the dislike of their own bodies. But this is also taking place in a country where one-third of the population is obese.

Perhaps the fourth or fifth anorexic young woman admitted to my care in that year was different. She was older, maybe 21, and she was not living with her upper-middle class parents. But she, it turned out, was also psychotic. Her refusal to eat, her body image distortions – these were symptoms of her schizophrenia.

And then there were others whose odd opinions of food, of eating, of chewing and masticating in public, were simply part of a larger pattern of excessive body consciousness, high anxiety, and obsessive-compulsive disorder.

For these latter two varieties of Anorexia we have specific treatments.

But the first and more common type remains something of a mystery. Much that has been written about it feels true: At a time in their lives when everything seems to be spiralling out of control (new expectations, responsibilities, complex relationships, body changes, hormone driven desires) at least she can control what and how much she eats. (Hence the benign form of protest at this age: "I've decided to be a vegetarian.") But starving to the point of stopping menstruation, to the point of retaining an 11 year-old body, might forestall the next complex and demanding developmental phase.

Unfortunately what can begin as a stubborn refusal to eat the large plate of food placed before this child by her (possibly overweight) mother can grow into a long and sometimes life-threatening struggle. And it can get quite crazy. On the pediatric and psychiatry wards these girls fill their pockets with rocks to fool the daily weigh-in; they do weight-loss exercises in front of the nursing station; they lie about food intake; they put the bread in their pockets along with the rocks; or slip away to regurgitate it. All the while remaining the "best little girls in town" and dutifully attending the Dietician to learn what nutrients the human body needs to survive.

And you have to ask yourself, what on earth is going on in the brain of someone, when told by doctors, dieticians, nurses, counsellors and her parents, that if she doesn't eat very soon she will die (and we are not necessarily talking about broccoli here, just one protein milkshake per day). And she still does not eat, though she is not suicidal and not, officially at least, insane.

But before it gets to that point, before you need to call for an appointment at the Eating Disorders Clinic, here is some advice: The most common form of anorexia in young teenage girls, and a few boys, would appear to be an expression of that thing discussed in previous chapters: Opposition. These girls are otherwise good, not foul of mouth, obedient to dress and curfew, but like all teens, attempting to individuate, to separate. **And this individuation is most easily achieved through defiance.** After all, defiance is the very first way the infant discovered that he or she is not an extension of the mother's nipple or hand. You just shake your head and say, "No."

And, as a sort of bonus, when you refuse to eat, you are not being an out-of-control teenager, a nasty or bad teenager, you are still being the best little girl in town, one to be concerned about, worried about, not scolded. So yes, much Anorexia starts as opposition, defiance, refusal, and then evolves into a power struggle between the very stubborn child and a mother who really cares precisely what food her child eats or doesn't eat.

It would be nice if you could encourage your daughter to rebel in other ways: say Goth clothing, bad music, poor hygiene, bad language, and refusal to do homework. But for a parent to suggest or encourage her child to choose alternative ways of rebelling, would be, of course, paradoxical. So your best option at this time is to make damn sure that eating - what she eats, when she eats, how much she eats - does **not** become an issue between you and does **not become a vehicle or the vehicle for a major power struggle between you.** As long as she is walking, talking, laughing, not

131

showing signs of malnutrition - leave it alone. To reassure yourself, watch a few movies from the 40's and 50's to remind yourself how skinny we all were back then. Opt out of that power struggle now. It is being maintained by your very interventions, no matter how well intended they are.

It is not a power struggle you can win head on. The refusal to eat, as Ghandi demonstrated, can defeat a nation, let alone a parent. If you do **not** make an issue of it, after she refuses to sit and eat the supper you prepared, she will probably sneak down from her room and forage in the refrigerator later.

An episode in Law and Order got it right. Detective Stabler's daughter was refusing to eat. He had a talk with Dr. Olivetti. Then he went home, and, upon entering the kitchen, said to his wife, "Come on, let's go out tonight. How about Italian?" Before his wife could answer, the daughter sitting at the table said, "I'm not eating Italian either." Then Stabler said, turning to his daughter: "You weren't invited."

Bulimia

The anorexic girls described above may also engage in some purging and vomiting, but a common form of Bulimia is a little different. The teen is somewhat older. She may have been overweight. And she is probably, at this time, recovering from her first break-up. She was in love as only a teenager can be, and she was rejected. Love pangs and hunger pangs feel about the same. They can be temporarily alleviated by binging. So she binges; the anguish is briefly eliminated, but then it returns in the form of self-loathing. She is fat; she will get fat; nobody will love her. It is difficult to self-induce vomiting the first time, but it gets much easier with practice.

132

A little of this is not a big deal. It may pass with time, with recovery from the lost love, with counselling. When prolonged it becomes dangerous, and a habit hard to break. It may be associated with depression and the treatment of this depression may fix the bulimia.

A new love interest may alleviate the problem. As might new interests, family counselling, and parental awareness, and some activity to replace the bingeing.

Sex and Pregnancy

The referral is made to the mental health clinic. The teenage girl (13, 14, 15, 16) is "out-of-control, running with a bad crowd, insisting on dating older boys, or hooking up with them, having mood swings, giving her parents "attitude". The waiting time for an appointment is four months.

The parents arrive for the appointment with their daughter in tow. She looks a little subdued. They look confused and perplexed. Before the interview begins the mother says, "Things have changed. Melanie is now two months pregnant."

Indeed they have changed, for the pregnancy trumps all. The girl and her parents are opposed to abortion. The original questions of "How can we bring our daughter under control?" and "Does she suffer from bipolar disorder?" are no longer central.

A few of these kids rise to the challenge. They mature quickly and take to being mothers of infants. A few of these families welcome the new infant into an extended family with the new mother and new grandmother and new grandfather happily sharing child-raising duties. Sometimes even the boy, the new father, takes to his responsibilities seriously.

But not often. Usually a world of trouble lies ahead.

So let's take this prevention of pregnancy seriously. It is not 'having sex too early in life' that will alter one's life drastically, but the consequences of having sex: pregnancy and STD's.

Teen boy-girl relationships have evolved. In one way for the better: some boys and girls seem now to be able to forge friendships, without sex interfering. But there is less attention paid to what once was quaintly called 'courtship' and later 'dating'. In fact, sometimes now when you ask a teen if he or she is 'dating' they don't know what you are talking about. They hang out together, boys and girls. Sometimes they 'hook up'. Sometimes they have 'friends with benefits.' And then when they do acquire a boyfriend or girlfriend they try to be together 24/7.

If you worry that your son or daughter is sexually active, they probably are. So you probably are a month or so late getting her to the family doctor to discuss birth control, and you probably are a month or two late putting some condoms in his sock drawer and having that talk. But do it and do it quickly.

Forge a relationship in which you can have these discussions openly and candidly, and get her on birth control, and tell him he doesn't have to hide his condoms. And while you are at it, have a frank discussion about STD's, protection, and the HPV vaccine. And though most teens can't imagine being thirty and thus can't imagine the long-term consequences of STD's, you can, and maybe on this subject you can impart your wisdom.

She's sixteen and dating (hooking up with) a nineteen year-old boy, who doesn't seem to have much of a future. You don't like this, and you would like it to stop. But if there is one area a parent needs to tread lightly it is with the impulse to try to break up a love relationship. Direct intervention can backfire, can bring about Romeo and Juliet rather than a Seinfeld episode, can force her to crawl out the window at night, run off to live with his parents, or an understanding aunt. You know how fleeting and unreliable passion can be. She does not. So if all other bases are covered: she is going to school, doing her homework, has a part-time job, not doing drugs…. then let the love relationship play out, but make sure she is taking her birth control pills, and make sure you are there to help pick up the pieces.

The fifteen year-old girl, to the parents' unease, had been seeing a nineteen-year-old boy about whom the parents knew very little. She had also been smoking marijuana and skipping school. While the parents were trying to deal with the latter problem, the boy was convicted of trafficking and sent to a Correctional Facility in another town. The girl tried to get her parents to drive her to see the boy during visiting hours. The parents saw this as an opportunity to end this relationship and refused to drive her. She was also grounded for skipping school. On Saturday she asked her parents if she could go outside to smoke. They agreed to this, but the father became suspicious. He followed his daughter outside and watched her walk to the end of their street. A car stopped. She got in. The father caught up to the car and discovered she had arranged with the parents of the nineteen year-old to be picked up a block from her home to go with them to visit the boy. The father was so incensed by this that he almost got into a fist-fight with the boy's father.

There are no easy answers to this one. Had the girl been, say, 12 to 14, more control, more authority, more intervention might work. At 17 you must grin and bear it and let it play out. At 15 or 16 years of age, it depends. It is a matter of strategy. What will bring about the best outcome? Treat this affair as if she is 13 and take control? Or does this risk losing your daughter? Or treat her as if she were older, make sure she is on birth control pills, and let it play out? In the anecdote above I might choose the paradoxical approach: the girl is extremely determined, stubborn, strong-willed. Opposing her relationship with the young criminal will probably push her into his arms. But how about accommodating it, driving her to see him, maybe insist she see him regularly, get to know his parents, meet the boy yourself? Remember how strong a need your adolescent has to rebel, to oppose, to distinguish herself from you. Your active involvement may quickly extinguish this passion.

But try to tell a father that.

Sexual Orientation and Gender Identity

This is a minefield for many parents from a variety of religious backgrounds and cultural expectations and I was going to avoid the topic until my niece, a family doctor and teacher of sexual education, told me I shouldn't. So here it is, simply and bluntly: There exists a five to ten percent chance your child will be gay, lesbian or bisexual, no matter your beliefs and wishes. She or he will begin to know this by age 12, give or take a couple of years. Before this age your child may have developed an intense attachment with a member of the same sex, but this might not be sexual in nature and may simply herald a life-long friendship. But as puberty begins and sexual urges develop your child will start to identify with one gender or the other, and have sexual feelings toward one gender or the other.

Some years ago a famous choreographer was being interviewed, and he told the story of how, age 14, while watching Gone With The Wind he found himself identifying with Scarlet O'Hara rather than Rhett Butler. Today it might be Bella instead of Edward Cullen, or vice versa. It is what Hollywood films set out to do: to make the viewer identify with the main characters, to experience the vicarious thrill of being Rhett Butler, or Bella, or Edward Cullen or Scarlet. How confusing, even terrifying this must be to any child raised in a homophobic environment. This teen may back away from relationships altogether. He may develop some self-loathing. He may become depressed. He certainly will try to keep his secret secret. He may over-compensate. The self-loathing may drive him or her to promiscuity.

Adolescence can be painful enough, embarrassing enough, without that particular identity confusion to deal with on one's own.

What can parents do? Well, long before the child reaches that age it would be nice if he or she had been raised in an inclusive family, an accepting family, had not been subjected to insensitive slurs or jokes, had listened to and perhaps participated in adult discussions of homosexuality and other differences, so that when that moment came he would know he can ask questions, admit to his feelings and interests and still be loved, supported and accepted.

It would also be nice if he or she were attending a school that practiced inclusion, had inclusive sex education programs, clubs for gays and lesbians to join. Many communities now have counselling programs specifically for Gay and Lesbian teens.

As parents you need to be in a position to be able to ask those questions, to reassure your teen that he or she is loved no matter the answer. You may have to tolerate, in your teen, a period of uncertainty, some trying both ways as it were. If the family environment was not accepting and inclusive before your child's discovery, you still have time to make it right, even if it means educating yourself, going for counselling yourself.

In real life we see all scenarios: the fully accepting and loving parents. The mother knows but the father doesn't. The father knows but the mother doesn't, even now he is 27 years old. They have come to accept the fact their son is gay. Her girlfriend has become a frequent visitor. Neither parent knows. The young man leads a double life. Today we see everything from full acceptance to complete denial and expulsion from the home.

Okay. I said I would make this simple and blunt. Your son or daughter may be gay or lesbian. You see the signs. Ask about it. Enter into a dialogue. Learn. Accept. Support. Look into helpful resources. Do not try to change or modify the direction this is going. You would be doing your child a great disservice.

On the other hand, the gay or lesbian teen is still a teen so everything else in this book still applies.

Drugs and Alcohol

We worry a lot about our teens using drugs but some studies show that alcohol is even more often used and abused by teenagers. It can be the drug of choice in certain age groups, even outstripping marijuana. So we need to worry about both.

Should we do the European thing? Introduce our kids to watered-down wine at an early age, in the appropriate social contexts? Teach them social drinking? Perhaps this works better than inadvertently enhancing the sweet illicit flavour of drinking by full and rabid prohibition. But, let's be honest, the rates of alcoholism and cirrhosis of the liver are pretty high in France.

Then there is the Dutch approach. Legalizing marijuana in The Netherlands has not done away with the problem of addictions, but it is safe to say **fewer Dutch teenagers attend school while stoned than do Canadian teenagers**. The adolescent response to information, to prohibitions, to the guidance of authority is complicated. (See first chapter)

138

Remember those days teens were herded into the school auditorium to watch films about the terrible medical consequences of smoking, complete with visuals of the nice pink lungs of non-smokers compared to the grotty lungs of smokers? Well, studies show that adolescent smoking **increases** after these lessons.

So with both drinking and drug use we need to be thoughtful and strategic. They will at some point try both. You can hope that first over-indulgence in alcohol will occur in a safe environment at an older age, say 17 or 18 rather than 13.

Your teens do need to know that drinking too much too fast can actually kill them. And they do need to know that if you ever catch them drinking and driving or riding in the car with a drunk teenage driver, you will "ground them for life".

Alcohol or marijuana use beyond the weekend party, say almost every day, may indicate some self-medicating for anxiety is happening. In this case there may be an underlying cause beyond adolescent perversity.

Both alcohol and drug use are occurring at an earlier age. I asked a 12 year-old girl how on earth she managed to acquire drugs, specifically cocaine. She told me, with a shrug, "You just go downtown, find a scruffy looking guy standing around on a corner, and go over and ask him if he's holding."

It is always a good rule of thumb to assume that whatever substance they admit to using, and how much they admit to using, that they are using other, more dangerous substances as well, and at least twice as much as they admit to.

The interview often goes something like this:

"So how often are you smoking marijuana?"

"Not much."

"How much is not much?"

"Hardly ever."

"So are we talking twice a day?"

"Naw. Not nearly that much."

"Once a week?"

"Maybe a little more than that."

"How about once a day and twice on the weekends?"

"Yeah, pretty much. But I'm trying to cut down."

"And how much does this cost you?"

"It doesn't cost me nothing. I get it from my buddies."

"Somebody's paying for it."

"Do they have to be here?" he says, nodding in the direction of his attentive parents.

"Absolutely."

The debate continues regarding marijuana. Teenagers know "reefer dangers" were exaggerated some years back. They argue it is a natural substance, unlike chemicals.

It may or may not actually cause brain changes; actually lead to more serious addictions. And it probably is no more, and possibly less, harmful than alcohol when used recreationally. (That means sharing a joint on Saturday night, and factoring in the sometimes tragic consequences of excess alcohol use).

But one thing is certain: Daily use of marijuana during that developmental phase when one should be challenged by life, relationships, information, new responsibilities, and feel some anxiety and pain, and learn by necessity to overcome these, to grow, and learn, to develop skills and competencies and new roles,

- daily marijuana use during this phase is simply bad. Who needs to learn and grow when they are engulfed in a marijuana haze?

The boy who smokes marijuana daily from age 16 to 20 arrives at age 20, still 16.

Then there is the rebound problem. Whenever a natural biological process is suppressed for any length of time by an externally derived substance, when that substance is stopped, the body overcompensates. It also may have shut down the mitochondrial factories that normally manufacture similar chemicals in times of need. Hence the deep depression that occurs when one ceases to use amphetamines, and the "living death" of the ex-heroin addict, and the anxiety attacks experienced by the marijuana user when he quits.

So how to approach this problem with a teenager? Simple "education about the evils of drug use" does not work. On the other hand, you need to be as informed as possible about the various substances available to your teenager, the street names for these things, and the various ways they are swallowed, inhaled and injected. It is all on the Internet.

As a parent you do have more real and ascribed power than any counsellor or drug program. So action is required on the part of parents, their involvement in any counselling or rehab program, and clarity of wishes, intentions, and expectations.

Perhaps when it is occurring between the ages of 10 and 14 you should simply put the child in lock-down. This means grounding with added supervision (the walk to school, noon hour, the walk home). Simply prevent the use of marijuana or other drugs, and provide alternative activities.

Age 17 and beyond, you have much less control (although surprisingly some 19 year-olds respond well to parental lockdown). But you can make sure you are not naïve, that you do not enable in any way, and that all your other expectations for citizenship in your household remain in place.

Drugs cost money. The money must come from someplace. Do not give him or her money for anything at all, even bus tickets, make sure he cannot get money from uncles and grandparents, and watch for stealing, and deal with stealing swiftly. When he does get busted, when he does get in trouble with the law, do not bail him out. I repeat, do not bail him out or pay for a lawyer. You may support him emotionally, help him problem solve, help him figure out how he can get himself past this point in his life, but it must be his responsibility. It can actually be a moment in his life when lessons are learned and new skills and confidence developed, if you do not do it for him.

So the rule is: **Do not enable in any way**. But don't give up on him or her. You will probably need a drug counsellor or mental health therapist to help you sort out the difference between enabling and being a loving, caring parent.

Don't just send your son or daughter to a drug counsellor or mental health counsellor. Attend as a family. It is a family problem, and as parents, as much as it hurts, as much as you want to avoid the pain, the confrontations, the accusations, you, as parents, have far more power to do something about the problem than any drug or rehabilitation counsellor. So attend as a family.

If you get down to the short strokes of tough love and you must throw him or her out of the house, having first tried less severe measures, leave the door open for your son or daughter to "reapply for citizenship." – the opportunity to come back, knock on the door, ask to be given another chance. You may have to repeat this cycle several times. Just don't give up.

There it is in a nutshell: Don't enable, but don't give up.

It is easier with most boys. No other family wants your lay-about pot-smoking son on their basement couch for very long. Chances are he will be knocking at your door within a week. But there is often someone out there (the misguided parents of her best friend, the 24 year-old dealer) who will be willing to take in your daughter. Alternative strategies may be required.

14, 15 and 16 are difficult ages. You are legally responsible, and morally responsible, so your tough-love options are limited. But you probably cannot exercise the kind of control you would like to exercise. Some 16 year-olds are ready for a little independence, some are not. Some still look like 12 year-old kids, others like 20 year-old football players.

So at that age you might find yourself in the somewhat paradoxical position of forbidding any drug use in the house, insisting on school attendance, allowing access to bed and refrigerator, making sure you are not enabling, while knowing full well (but not liking) the fact that he or she is using marijuana regularly outside the home. Again, it has to be paid for; it will eventually bring on grief and failure. Attend a counsellor, work on the problem, wait for the opportunity to act.

Simply attending a counsellor as a family can bring about a full disclosure of drug use, and a plan to reduce and quit. But make it a family affair.

It is often said that addicts don't stop using and alcoholics don't stop drinking until they decide to, or have hit "rock bottom." But it seems more obviously true, that as humans indulging in this kind of behaviour, we don't stop unless and until **we have to**.

That moment of **"have to"** can be brought about by a medical event, a loved one's demand, a boss threatening termination, the loss or threatened loss of your children, or an arrest and appearance in court.

And for a teenager, the "have to" moment can be brought about by the actions of parents. So, again, attend the counsellor, family doctor, psychologist, or psychiatrist as a family.

If this particular counsellor won't see you as a family, or talk to you about your son or daughter, for whatever reasons, find one who will.

It is quite understandable that parents often take their teenager to the counsellor, family doctor, psychologist or psychiatrist, with the sometimes spoken, but often tacit request of, "Please take him, work with him, fix him, and then send him back to us." But the counsellor can't take away the car keys, shut down the internet, remove the cell phone, withhold money, insist on school attendance, monitor school attendance, search his room, lock the door at curfew, stop doing his washing, stop driving him to the mall. But you can, with the counsellor's help.

***

144

Other Titles from Bridgeross Communications:

After Her Brain Broke: Helping My Daughter Recover Her Sanity, by Susan Inman 978-0-9810037-8-8, 2010, 168 pages, $18.95, distributed by Ingram.

> - "A model for other families. Highly recommended" Dr. E Fuller Torrey, author of *Surviving Schizophrenia* and former advisor to the National Alliance For the Mentally Ill.

Schizophrenia: Medicine's Mystery Society's Shame, by Marvin Ross, 978-0-9810037-0-2, 2008, 188 pages, $19.95, distributed by Ingram and QBI

> - "a powerful resource for anyone looking for answers and insight into the world of mental illness." Schizophrenia Digest Magazine.

The Brush, The Pen and Recovery, A 33 minute documentary on schizophrenia distributed by Moving Images, Vancouver, BC

> - "profoundly moving, educational and hopeful." Eufemia Fanteti author and performer of "My Own Private Etobicoke", Toronto, ON .

My Schizophrenic Life: The Road to Recovery From Mental Illness, Sandra Yuen MacKay, 978-0-9810037-9-5, 210 pages, 2010 $19.95, distributed by Ingram

> - "Important book (that) should be read by anyone wanting to understand how someone can recover from schizophrenia. Remarkably compelling" - Library Journal